# TEAM PERFORMANCE INVENTORY

## PARTICIPANT WORKBOOK

## Darlene Davis and Wayne Davis

Pfeiffer
A Wiley Imprint
www.pfeiffer.com

Published by Pfeiffer
An Imprint of Wiley
989 Market Street, San Francisco, CA 94103-1741
www.pfeiffer.com

For additional copies/bulk purchases of this book in the U.S. please contact 800-274-4434.

Pfeiffer books and products are available through most bookstores. To contact Pfeiffer directly call our Customer Care Department within the U.S. at 800-274-4434, outside the U.S. at 317-572-3985, fax 317-572-4002, or visit www.pfeiffer.com.

Pfeiffer also publishes its books in a variety of electronic formats. Some content that appears in print may not be available in electronic books.

ISBN: 978-0-7879-8669-8

Acquiring Editor: Martin Delahoussaye
Director of Development: Kathleen Dolan Davies
Production Editor: Dawn Kilgore
Editor: Rebecca Taff
Editorial Assistant: Julie Rodriquez
Manufacturing Supervisor: Becky Morgan

Printed in the United States of America
*Printing*   10 9 8 7 6 5 4 3 2 1

# CONTENTS

# 1

# The Benefits of Teams

# The Stages of Team Performance

## Teams—Today's Reality

Now, more than ever before, organizations are creating teams—cross-functional teams, virtual teams, self-directed teams, process-improvement teams, project teams, and numerous ad-hoc, hybrid teams to implement their business strategy, conduct day-to-day operations, and manage their relationships.

## Team Performance—Today's Challenge

However, creating and assembling a team is only the beginning. Just as with any building project, teams need plans and blueprints, processes and tools, and the necessary competencies, attitudes, and leadership to perform effectively. The challenge is to develop the needed team-building knowledge, skills, and training that drives team effectiveness. Unfortunately, and quite frequently, teams are left to fend on their own with few resources and little support to help them reach effective levels of performance.

## What Is a Team?

"A team is a group of individuals who must work interdependently in order to attain their individual and organizational objectives."

*Katzenbach and Smith, 1993*

According to Reilly and Jones (1974) and Katzenbach and Smith (1993), there are four essential elements to a team:

1. The group must have a charter or reason for working together.

> ### Team
>
> A team is a number of people with complementary skills who are committed to a common purpose, approach, and set performance goals for which they hold themselves mutually accountable.
>
> The essence of a team is a common commitment. Without it, the members of the group perform as individuals; with it, they become a powerful unit of collective performance.

3

2. Members of the group must be interdependent—they need each other's experience, ability, and commitment in order to arrive at mutual goals.

3. Group members must be committed to the idea that working together as a group leads to more effective decisions than working in isolation.

4. The group must be accountable as a functioning unit within a larger organizational context. (Reilly & Jones, 1974)

When the team's performance or accomplishments surpass the capabilities of the individual group members, synergy occurs. The team's unique combination of talents, knowledge, and experience is greater than the aggregation of the individual contributions. The ideas of one member can often trigger a response from another member in a way that they never would have thought of independently. The energy of one individual can spur others on when their own vitality diminishes.

In his article "Social Facilitation," Zajonc (1963, p. 269–274) says: "Synergy can take either physical or cognitive forms. The physical presence of others is often affecting, so more work is accomplished. Even ants work harder when there is more than one of them on the job." In the cognitive sense, synergy emerges when a type of collective intelligence and shared memory begins to develop as the group matures. Also, synergy can play an important role for those team members who are energized through interaction with others.

# The Benefits of Teams

## How Teams Benefit Organizations

Teaming promotes knowledge sharing and generates a variety of approaches and possible solutions. The age-old cliché, "two heads are better than one," reflects the belief that, when individuals unite, they consistently produce solutions to problems that are more creative and make better decisions than individuals working on their own.

An example could be a talent acquisition team that is responsible for staffing the organization with the best match of skills and cultural fit. The team's makeup typically includes recruiters, human resources, compensation and benefits, diversity, planners, and operations. The team's challenge is to interpret the company's requirements and synchronize them with market realities. Each team member plays a vital role in the process. A role that is uniquely performed in a team setting.

> "In the ideal team, each member performs his or her function in such a way that it dovetails with that of other team members to enable the team to achieve its goals. By this collaboration, the whole becomes greater than the sum of its parts."
>
> *Pell, 1999*

## How Teams Benefit Individuals

Working on a team can challenge its members to go beyond normative behaviors and achieve their maximum potential. Being part of a team provides opportunities to broaden an individual's perspective, widen and deepen people's knowledge, and master new skills in ways that might not be available to an individual contributor. Working collectively to set goals and solve problems, brainstorming to generate creative ideas and options, and sharing responsibilities are some of the many benefits of the team experience.

A satisfying team experience creates a sense of belonging. Studies show that many people learn better through interacting with one another than when working alone.

Since a significant portion of a professional's job is relationship-oriented, an individual's teamability is critical to his or her long-term career success. No matter how competent or ambitious people are, if they want to be successful as team leaders or players, they must be able to establish and maintain productive relationships with others.

A high-performing team reflects favorably on the individual team members and increases their visibility in the organization.

Organizations depend on a matrix of interlocking skills and capabilities, both individually and collectively. Today, interdependence is a business reality. For your team to be successful requires both team and individual accountability. Accountability drives team performance levels higher than individuals can achieve themselves, even when performing at their personal best.

# Team Building: A Continuing Process

Team building is not a one-time event. It is a continuing process that begins by introducing and then reinforcing both team-tasking skills and interpersonal behavioral skills as the team develops and matures.

> "The process of team building is critical to the development of successful teams and accomplishment of team goals."
>
> *Kormanski and Mozenter, 2002*

Although team building demands attention and hard work, there are significant benefits for developing teaming skills and serious consequences for not doing so. Those benefits and consequences are summarized in Table 1.

**Table 1. Team Building: The Business Case**

| Positive Outcomes When Team Building Takes Place | Negative Consequences of Not Doing or Delaying Team Building |
|---|---|
| Team goals are understood in the context of organizational goals. | Performance and quality suffer due to unclear goals and direction. |
| Techniques to improve team performance are learned and adopted. | Bad habits and disruptive behaviors go unchecked. |
| Improved understanding and communication among members is evident. | Differences are not reconciled and conflicts are not resolved. |
| Roles and responsibilities are clarified and aligned. | There is an overlap of responsibilities or a few members do most of the work. |
| Information is shared and exchanged among members. | Information hoarding negatively affects problem solving and decision making. |
| Common commitment and increased loyalty begin to bond the team together. | Members become complacent and lack commitment to the team. |
| Stretch assignments drive stretch accomplishments. | Status quo and stagnation become modus operandi. |
| Boost in synergy, enthusiasm, and esprit de corps. | Loss of creativity, respect, trust, and motivation demoralizes the team. |
| A shared purpose and mutual accountability—a "we" versus "me" environment. | Members prioritize personal objectives at the expense of the success of the team. |

# II

# The Four Stages of Team Performance

# Introduction to the Four Stages

From extensive research in group dynamics and the process of team building (Francis & Young, 1979; Solomon, 2002), a great deal is known about how teams perform. Numerous studies on group behavior are available and provide a strong foundation of knowledge about the team experience (Shultz, 1958). Theory on team development, particularly as it relates to performance, proposes that teams, as individuals, pass through predictable stages over time (Tuckman, 1965, 1977).

## Team Performance

The *Team Performance Inventory* identifies four stages of team performance and their four concurrent styles of team leadership. The four stages of team performance are defined as Initiating, Conflicting, Stabilizing, and Performing.

Each of the four stages is defined by its unique characteristics and attributes, its key traits of tasks and relationships, its role of leaders, role of members, and the development activities and action steps to improve the team's performance including:

- Stage description
- General characteristics
- What members want to know
- Leader's role
- Members' roles
- Team action steps to be accomplished
- Indicators of open items
- Key trait of task outcome
- Key trait of relationship outcome
- Suggested development activities
- Exercises and resources

# Team Leadership

The four leadership styles are defined as Directing, Coaching, Facilitating, and Delegating. The Directing leadership style is the preferred style for the Initiating stage, the Coaching leadership style is the preferred style for the Conflicting stage, the Facilitating leadership style is the preferred style for the Stabilizing stage, and the Delegating leadership style is the preferred style for the Performing stage.

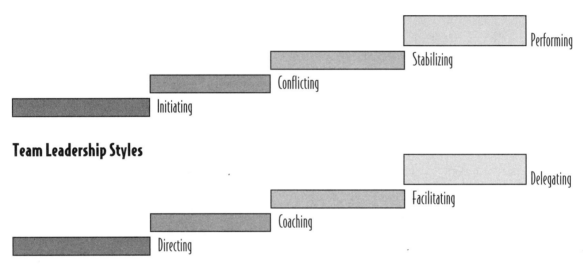

**Figure 2.1.**   Team Performance Stages

# Key Dimensions of Team Performance: Task and Relationship

Each stage, Initiating, Conflicting, Stabilizing, and Performing, overlays and reflects two dimensions or orientations of team performance; task and relationship.

1. **Task.** The task dimension is doing the work the team is entrusted to do. This includes setting goals and objectives, designing implementation plans, developing budgets, determining roles and responsibilities, solving problems, and making decisions.

2. **Relationship.** The relationship dimension refers to the interaction necessary to get things done. It speaks to the human side of the dynamics that occur in the group, how the members act together to complete the task. This component addresses the effectiveness of the relationship and interface among team members. It pertains to the feelings, behaviors, and problems members have with one another in the group. Developing mission and values, generating open communication, giving constructive feedback, and building trust are examples of the relationship dimension.

Looking at team development from this perspective will emphasize the importance not only of the two dimensions—task and relationship—but will also provide a common language through which team members can explore the emerging characteristics and parameters of the group.

It is the convergence of task productivity and relationship well-being (see Figure 2.2) that results in effective team performance. Thus, a team's effectiveness can be measured by its ability to accomplish its objectives and to work together in a way that satisfies the team members' interpersonal needs at the same time.

When a team is over-focusing on the task without concern or attention to interpersonal relations, tension and conflict may occur. Likewise, over-focusing on relationships may result in strong personal interactions, but potentially sacrifices task accomplishment. To be successful at both task and relationships, a cohesive integration of these two key dimensions is needed.

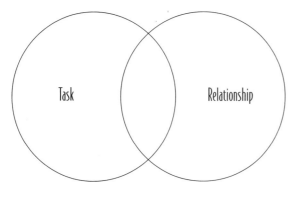

**Figure 2.2.** Effective Team Performance: Task and Relationship

13

## The Correlation of Task Functions and Relationship Attributes

Figure 2.3 illustrates how the stages of the team's relationship attributes parallel with the team's task functions. When a team moves through the task functions and relationship attributes simultaneously, the growth and regression in one dimension influence the behavior and development in the other. In order for the team to advance in both task and relationship stages at the same time, specific action steps must be taken.

## Team Development and Growth

Each stage of team performance has its unique challenges that must be understood and addressed, as well as specific steps to accomplish before the group can fully progress to the next stage. Teams can stagger, idle, and even stop at any stage. The progression is dependent on various factors:

- The members' relationship and task readiness
- The leader's ability to adapt the appropriate leader style for each stage
- The complexity of the task
- The organization's backing and support
- Available and committed resources

To be a wholly functioning team depends on how effectively the relationship and task aspects are managed, synthesized (integrated), and synchronized (matched).

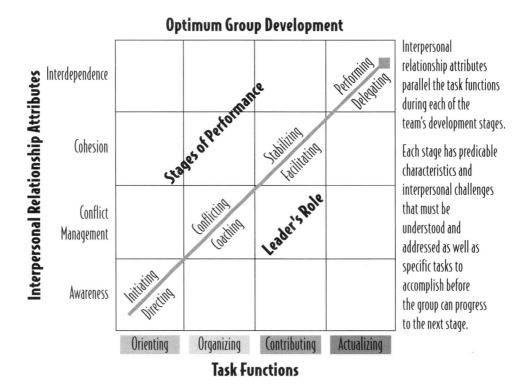

**Figure 2.3.**    Relationship Attributes and Task Functions

## Individual Commitment

For teams to maximize their performance requires that each team member make a serious and concerted effort to grow in both interpersonal relations and task accomplishment. Even one or two members who are unwilling to commit to a shared responsibility for the team's initiatives can sabotage the team's performance and its ability to execute its goals. Being a contributing team player many times necessitates moving out of one's comfort zone, taking risks, and making behavioral and attitude changes. To do so can be highly rewarding. To do otherwise can be career limiting.

# Characteristics of the Four Stages

## Initiating Stage

The Initiating stage is a stage of transition from individual to team status. Initiating takes place when the team members first come together. At this stage, little structure is in place; purpose, goals, roles, and relationships are unclear. When a team is at the beginning stage and still unclear about tasks and relationships, members are exploring the boundaries of acceptable group behavior.

## General Characteristics

In the Initiating stage of team development:

- Members become acquainted with each other and begin to consider the tasks that are to be accomplished.

- Members take note, size up, and make comparisons of similarities and differences.

- First impressions are formed that can be lasting (this will change as members work on building their team).

- People want to avoid conflict and controversy, and generally pay lip service (telling others what they want to hear).

- People are polite and guarded are willing to go along with ideas as presented unless someone suggests something that is too extreme.

- There are hidden agendas, with superficial, non-authentic communication and relationships.

- Goals are unclear, and members are dependent on a directing leadership style.

## What Members Want to Know

During the Initiating stage, team members want to know where they fit, their roles, and what is expected of them, that is, how the skills and knowledge they bring will be used and valued and what commitments are required. They may wonder:

- Why are we here?

- What will we be doing?

- How will we get things done?

- What are our goals?
- Do I want to be a part of this team?
- What's in it for me?
- Will I be accepted as a member?
- What price must I pay to belong to this team?
- How competent are the team members?
- Who is the leader?
- Is the leader competent?

> **Feelings and Emotions**
>
> - Excitement
> - Pride in being selected
> - Confusion and testing the waters
> - Uncertainty and anxiety about the job ahead

## Leader's Role (Directing Style)

The leader's role in the Initiating stage is to use a Directing style of leadership. Leaders who have a preference or tendency for this style will be comfortable and find it easy to adapt. Those who don't have an inclination for this style will need to make an extra effort to learn and apply the attributes of the Directing style in order to be more effective leaders for a team in the Initiating stage. Prominent aspects of the Directing style include:

- Providing structure, clear task direction, and driving the team process
- Allowing get-acquainted time
- Encouraging participation
- Urging people out of their comfort zones
- Insisting on effective listening
- Not assuming the appearance of harmony is real
- Asserting power

## Team Members' Roles

Members' roles are key to the team's success. At each stage of team performance, members' talents, behaviors, and attitudes are vital. As a team member, your role during the Initiating stage is:

Place a check (✔) in the box for each of the areas below that you would like to personally develop.

- ❑ Asking questions to clarify team's initial purpose and tasks
- ❑ Having patience with the process
- ❑ Listening actively
- ❑ Being open to new ideas
- ❑ Resisting pre-judgment and preconceived attitudes

## Action Steps to Be Accomplished

Following are the action steps that the team needs to accomplish in the Initiating stage in order to advance to the next stage. As you will note, some of the actions are behavioral and will take time before they become embedded as common team practices. Allow time for the behaviors to change and mature.

Place a check (✓) in the box for each of the areas below that you feel your team would benefit by addressing and developing.

- ❑ Building a common purpose
- ❑ Identifying interests and values
- ❑ Assessing talent resources (i.e., *who* has *what* to contribute)
- ❑ Determining stakeholders' and clients/customers' expectations
- ❑ Developing goals that are aligned with the organization's strategic intent
- ❑ Discussing individual and team expectations
- ❑ Sharing relevant information
- ❑ Encouraging interactive dialogue
- ❑ Providing structure and direction to team issues
- ❑ Engaging in team activities that build trust and open communication

## Indicators of Open Items

What are the signs that will tell you that things might not be going as planned? What are the earmarks and red flags of stagnation or reversion? The following are indicators that there are open items that may need to be addressed and resolved:

- Members work in disarray.
- Team members know little about each other (values, interests, and motivators).
- Lack of recognition of potential skills, abilities, and contributions of team members.
- Expectations are unmet, so people become upset or withdraw.
- It is unclear how individuals will be rewarded and recognized for participating in the team.

When new members join the team during later stages, this is a time to take a pulse check and revisit the Action Steps to Be Accomplished.

## Key Traits

Key traits are signs the team is making progress in task accomplishment and/or interpersonal relationships along the performance continuum. When you see these traits in your team, you will know you are moving forward.

### Key Trait of Task Outcome

*Definition:* Members are beginning to understand the task, its implications, and expectations.

### Key Trait of Relationship Outcome

*Awareness:* Members are becoming cognizant of the personalities, behaviors, and attitudes of others.

# Notes

_____

_____

_____

_____

_____

_____

_____

_____

_____

_____

_____

_____

_____

_____

_____

_____

_____

_____

_____

_____

# Conflicting Stage

In the Conflicting stage, team members realize that the task can be more difficult than they imagined. Conflicting begins as the team starts to define roles and responsibilities. During this stage, the focus is on both task and relationship. The team is vulnerable at this point because of conflicting opinions concerning tasks, processes, and goals, and feelings of confusion and incompetence are common. Members may be second-guessing their ability to do a good job.

Some members may become dissatisfied and express discomfort, not only with what the team is doing and how, but also with the leader's role and style of leadership. True personalities begin to emerge, and tension among members is common.

Don't try to skip or shortcut this stage. A team that does not go through the Conflicting stage won't learn how to deal with and resolve disputes. It becomes passive, does not incorporate all of the strengths of its members, and fails to go through the sometimes painful, yet necessary, process of becoming truly creative and effective.

This is considered the most crucial stage that the team must work through. The result of the Conflicting stage is either a united group that is ready to become organized or a split group, with some people withdrawing from taking on active responsibilities (that is, fight or flight).

## General Characteristics

In the Conflicting stage of team development:

- Issues are power, control, leadership, and problem solving.
- Infighting abounds and conflict cannot be avoided during this phase.
- Team members react toward leadership with counterproductive behaviors.
- Coalitions or cliques may form.
- Competition is high among team members.
- Confusion about tasks, roles, and assignments exists.
- Communication deteriorates; team members are uncertain about how to deal with issues openly.
- There is a general lack of trust.
- Personal attacks are common.

## What Members Want to Know

Team members want to know where they fit, their roles, and what is expected of them. They want to know how the skills and knowledge they bring will be used and valued as a member of the team, and they want to know what commitments are required. They may wonder:

- What are the expectations of me and other team members?
- Who is going to be responsible for what?

- What are the rules? What are the parameters?
- How will I seek my autonomy?
- How much control will I have over the others?
- How much control will others try to have over me?
- Whom do I support? Who supports me?
- How much influence do I have in this team?
- How will I be rewarded and recognized?

> **Feelings and Emotions**
>
> Confusion, Anxiety
> Anger, Frustration
> Agitation, Impatience
> Little team spirit

## Leader's Role (Coaching Style)

The leader's role in the Conflicting stage is a Coaching style of leadership. Leaders who have a preference or tendency for this style will be comfortable and find it easy to adapt. Those who don't have an inclination for this style will need to make an extra effort to learn and apply the attributes of the Coaching style in order to be more effective leaders. Prominent aspects of the Coaching style include:

- Encouraging members to ask questions for clarification
- Promoting bi-directional communication
- Actively listening
- Raising difficult issues
- Acknowledging, not fearing conflict, and striving to manage it constructively
- Reminding team members they can agree to disagree
- Encouraging members to assume more task responsibility
- Coaching the team through struggles and guiding it toward consensus
- Actively supporting and reinforcing positive team behavior
- Meeting with disruptive personalities privately, discussing and resolving issues
- Coaching accountability

## Team Members' Roles

Members' roles are key to the team's success. At each stage of team performance, members' talents, behaviors, and attitudes are vital. As a team member, your role during the Conflicting stage is critical.

Place a check (✔) in the boxes below for each of the areas you would like to personally develop.

- ❑ Seeking clarity about purpose, roles, and responsibilities
- ❑ Risking self-disclosure
- ❑ Initiating ideas

❑ Respecting diversity of team members

❑ Accepting that conflict is inevitable and finding ways to use it effectively, rather than avoiding, suppressing, or ignoring it

❑ Speaking only for yourself

❑ Helping the team reach consensus on purpose, goals, and roles

## Action Steps to Be Accomplished

Following are the action steps that need to be accomplished in the Conflicting stage in order to advance to the next stage. As you will note, some of the actions are behavioral and will take time before they become embedded as common team practices. Allow time for the behaviors to change and mature.

Place a check (✓) in the box for each of the areas below you feel your team would benefit by addressing and developing.

❑ Ensuring Conflicting stage issues are addressed

❑ Encouraging an open flow of communication

❑ Supporting collaborative team efforts

❑ Involving everyone in the discussion; inquiring into differences

❑ Clarifying roles and responsibilities

❑ Discussing individual and mutual accountability

❑ Establishing and building ground rules, (i.e., rules of behavior—what is and what is not appropriate)

❑ Discussing and concurring on how you will disagree

❑ Learning to address topics that are potentially embarrassing or threatening

❑ Discussing and agreeing on a decision-making processes

❑ Defining a rewards and recognition structure

## Indicators of Open Items

What are the signs that will tell us things might not be going as planned? What are the earmarks and red flags of stagnation or reversion? The following are indicators that there are open items that need to be addressed and resolved:

• Communication breakdown

• Unclear roles and responsibilities

• Failure to discuss potentially threatening or embarrassing topics

• Differing views that are not encouraged or respected

• Inability to deal with conflict constructively

• Dissatisfaction with how decisions are made

When new members join the team during later stages, this is a time to take a pulse check and revisit the Action Steps to Be Accomplished from earlier stages.

## Key Traits

Key traits are signs the team is making progress in task accomplishment and/or interpersonal relationships along the performance continuum. When you see these traits in your team, you will know you are moving forward.

### Key Trait of Task Outcome

*Organization:* Members are adopting approaches and practices on how the task should be planned, organized, and implemented.

### Key Trait of Relationship Outcome

*Conflict Management:* Members are moving beyond opposition and disagreement and seeking constructive and affirming relationships.

## Notes

_____

_____

_____

_____

_____

_____

_____

_____

_____

_____

_____

_____

_____

_____

_____

_____

# Stabilizing Stage

In the Stabilizing stage, team members understand and accept the team's ground rules, their roles on the team, and the individuality of fellow members. Stabilizing is the stage in which people become more comfortable working with one another. You will begin to see cooperation over competition and more acceptance. Communication seems more open and honest, and team members are more at ease in giving and receiving feedback.

Efforts are made to determine what standards of performance are acceptable. Members are working on common performance issues. As team members become more comfortable working together, they have more time and energy to spend on the tasks and are able to make significant progress.

## General Characteristics

In the Stabilizing stage of team development:

- Teams have sufficient resources to accomplish the task.
- Members perform their roles and responsibilities with acquired proficiency.
- Appreciation builds.
- Increased interaction, cooperation, and collaboration are obvious.
- Members care about each other's well-being and support individuals in periods of difficultly.
- Cross-functional relationships have developed through interdependent behavior.
- Members enjoy their work and team interaction.
- Trust, the most vital ingredient in team dynamics, begins to unfold.

## What Members Want to Know

Team members want to know where they fit, their roles, and what is expected of them. They want to know how the skills and knowledge they bring will be used and valued as a member of the team. And they want to know what commitments are required. Team members may wonder:

- Is quality really going to be a priority?
- Do we really mean what we say when we set deadlines?
- Is it okay to miss meetings?
- What do I need to do more of, less of, differently?
- How do others see me?

> **Feelings and Emotions**
>
> Relief that the situation is improving
> Acceptance, feeling respected and valued for strengths, unique talents, and differences
> Positive energy with increased productivity

## Leader's Role (Facilitating Style)

The leader's role in the Stabilizing stage is a Facilitating style of leadership. Leaders who have a preference or tendency for this style will be comfortable and find it easy to adapt. Those who don't have an inclination for this style will need to make an extra effort to learn and apply the attributes of the Facilitating style in order to be more effective leaders. Prominent aspects of the Facilitating style include:

- Communicating; sharing ideas and information
- Reinforcing the vision of what the team can become
- Discouraging groupthink and encouraging diverse opinions and disparate ideas
- Initiating personal development plans for team members
- Using a Facilitating style to involve the team in decision making
- Encouraging wide participation and safeguarding less-heard viewpoints
- Reinforcing positive teaming behavior
- Requesting and accepting constructive criticism and feedback

## Team Members' Roles

Members' roles are key to the team's success. At each stage of team performance, members' talents, behaviors, and attitudes are vital. Place a check (✔) in the box below for each of the areas you would like to personally develop.

- ❏ Preparing for and contributing during team meetings
- ❏ Voicing both opposing and confirming viewpoints
- ❏ Buying into objectives and activities
- ❏ Communicating, communicating, and communicating
- ❏ Requesting and accepting feedback
- ❏ Self-reinforcing team ground rules
- ❏ Committing to a "no surprises" contract with other team members
- ❏ Working proactively for the benefit of the team
- ❏ Demonstrating active listening and a willingness to change
- ❏ Building trust by honoring commitments
- ❏ Taking responsibility for a professional development plan with stretch goals that align with the team's goals and the organization's strategy

## Action Steps to Be Accomplished

Following are the action steps that the team needs to accomplish in the Stabilizing stage in order to advance to the next stage. As you will note, some of the actions are behavioral and will take time before they become embedded as common team practices. Allow time for the behaviors to change and mature.

Place a check (✓) in the box for each of the areas you feel your team would benefit by addressing and developing.

- ❏ Talking openly about issues and concerns
- ❏ Giving positive and constructive feedback
- ❏ Developing processes for information sharing, feedback, and resource allocation
- ❏ Having open forums on tasks and relationships, both internal and external; negotiating where appropriate
- ❏ Building on positive behaviors and changing unsupportive behaviors
- ❏ Supporting consensus decision-making efforts
- ❏ Assuring that team goals are clear, specific, and measurable and that all team members accept the goals and their roles in achieving them
- ❏ Performing roles and responsibilities with proficiency
- ❏ Setting high expectations and developing the skills and knowledge required to help the team do what it says it will do

## Indicators of Open Items

What are the signs that will tell us things might not be going as planned? What are the earmarks and red flags of stagnation or reversion? The following are indicators that there are open items that need to be addressed and resolved during the Stabilizing stage.

- Team fails to embrace ground rules
- Lack of trust and openness
- No congruence in how the group is to work together
- No established channels for giving and receiving feedback
- Work is not done on time or is inadequate

When new members join the team during later stages, this is a time to take a pulse check and revisit the Action Steps to Be Accomplished from earlier stages.

## Key Traits

Key traits are signs the team is making progress in task accomplishment and/or interpersonal relationships along the performance continuum. When you see these traits in your team, you will know you are moving forward.

### Key Trait of Task Outcome

*Contribution:* Members hold each other accountable to meet deadlines, adhere to rules, and meet performance standards.

### Key Trait of Relationship Outcome

*Cohesion:* Members participate openly, provide encouragement and support, and speak of their team with pride.

# Notes

_____

_____

_____

_____

_____

_____

_____

_____

_____

_____

_____

_____

_____

_____

_____

_____

_____

_____

_____

_____

_____

_____

_____

_____

_____

_____

_____

_____

_____

_____

## Performing Stage

In the Performing stage, team members have gained insight into personal and team processes and have a good understanding of each other's strengths and weaknesses. They are able to work through group conflict, and members have learned how to resolve differences. They have developed close attachments with each other and have a strong identity with the team.

Now the team is working collectively toward common milestones and accomplishments. Collaboration and synergy pervade. The team is flexible and is able to anticipate and plan for change. Performing occurs because individuals feel their contributions are valued and thus eagerly contribute to the team's success. There is a strong interdependence among team members, not only for expertise and information, but also for reciprocal support and backup. The team has become an effective, cohesive unit; they can begin performing. Due to various factors, many teams do not achieve the Performing stage.

## General Characteristics

In the Performing stage of team development:

- Team members share responsibility for goals.
- High openness, support, and trust are obvious.
- There is a team identity: "We're all in this together."
- New ideas are being generated.
- New perspectives are sought and adopted.
- Team members achieve interdependence (work well together, achieving more together than they would as individuals).
- There are no surprises.
- There's little waste, an intolerance for poor performance, and very efficient team processes and operations.
- It is okay to risk confrontation and exposure.
- Team members feel very motivated and productive.
- High-quality services, products, and outputs are evident.
- The team networks throughout the organization and creates partnerships with other teams.

## What Members Want to Know

Team members want to know where they fit, their roles, and what is expected of them. They want to know how the skills and knowledge they bring will be used and valued as a member of the team. And they want to know what commitments are required. They may wonder:

- How will we know when we are successful?

- What can we do to continue the momentum?

- How can we be better tomorrow than we are today?

- What can we do to better meet the needs of our internal and external clients/customers?

- What can we do to improve our influence in the organization?

### Feelings and Emotions

"We" versus "me" orientation
Pride in team
High empathy and high trust
Objective outlooks
Appreciation of strengths and
    limitations
Strong sense of congruency and
    synergy
Satisfaction increases as the team
    achieves high performance

## Leader's Role (Delegating Style)

The leader's role in the Performing stage is a Delegating style of leadership. Leaders who have a preference or tendency for this style will be comfortable and find it easy to adapt. Those who don't have an inclination for this style will need to make an extra effort to learn and apply the attributes of the Delegating style in order to be a more effective leader. Prominent aspects of the Delegating style include:

- Ensuring team is up-to-date on organization strategy and business initiatives, current and relevant industry and business trends

- Encouraging thinking outside the margins

- Emphasizing quality work and outcomes

- Utilizing each member's unique talents and encouraging stretch assignments

- Delegating leadership roles in the team based on who does what the best

- Being selective of new team members; training to maintain the team's camaraderie and esprit de corps

- Continuing to evaluate the team against high performance goals

- Remaining alert to the team's need for skill development, conflict management, attitude improvement, and trust building

- Focusing on purpose, interdependent relationships, and conditions that shift the stages

- Marketing the team's talents and progress to others outside the team

## Team Members' Roles

Members' roles are key to the team's success. At each stage of team performance, members' talents, behaviors, and attitudes are vital. As a team member, place a check (✓) in the box for each of the areas you would like to personally develop.

❑ Having a sense of individual responsibility for the team's success

❑ Deferring to team needs; keeping team objectives in the forefront while managing personal precedence

❑ Introducing and cultivating new ideas

❑ Committing to mutual accountability

❑ Applying positive pressure to assure the team achieves effective and satisfying results

❑ Taking full responsibility for tasks and relationships

❑ Eliminating duplication of efforts by acknowledging and using each member's unique contributions to the team's objective

❑ Keeping up with the latest trends and developments in your field and industry

❑ Presenting the team's mission, goals, plans, and purpose energetically to others outside the team

## Action Steps to Be Accomplished

Following are the action steps that the team needs to accomplish in the Performing stage. As you will note, some of the actions are behavioral and will take time before they become embedded as common team practices. Allow time for the behaviors to change and mature.

Place a check (✓) in the box for each of the areas you feel your team would benefit by addressing and developing.

❑ Focusing on the big picture and pragmatic deliverables and solutions

❑ Bringing ideas to reality

❑ Evaluating processes and procedures to determine potential areas for improvement

❑ Communicating views and feelings

❑ Delegating freely within the team

❑ Continuously raising the bar

❑ Setting fresh and challenging goals

❑ Packaging our success factors as a repeatable process

## Indicators of Open Items

What are the signs that will tell us things might not be going as planned? What are the earmarks and red flags of stagnation or reversion? The following are indicators that there are open items that need to be addressed and resolved:

• Lack of periodic reviews using feedback, metrics, and internal and external analysis to evaluate progress and make improvements

• Failure to commit quality time to the team

- Members do not present the team's goals and plans to external others similarly
- Inability or lack of desire to initiate innovative ideas and change

When new members join the team during later stages, this is a time to take a pulse check and revisit the Action Steps to Be Accomplished from earlier stages.

## Key Traits

Key traits are signs the team is making progress in task accomplishment and/or interpersonal relationships along the performance continuum. When you see these traits in your team, you will know you are moving forward.

### Key Trait of Task Outcome

*Actualizing Solutions:* Members are doing the right things right. Creativity and innovation are evident in outcomes and results.

### Key Trait of Relationship Outcome

*Interdependence:* Members rely on each other for constructive feedback. There is a strong bond among members and a sense of community.

# Notes

_____

_____

_____

_____

_____

_____

_____

_____

_____

_____

_____

_____

_____

_____

_____

_____

_____

_____

_____

_____

_____

_____

_____

_____

_____

# Turning Point

For teams who have reached the Performing stage, there is no time to rest on their laurels. During the Performing stage, teams may come to a crossroads (see Figure 2.4) where (1) they lose momentum, a sense of purpose, become comfortable and complacent, stagnate and decline or (2) they renew their mission by creating fresh opportunities and developing challenging team goals that align with organizational objectives. They value their interdependence and work hard to stay out in front.

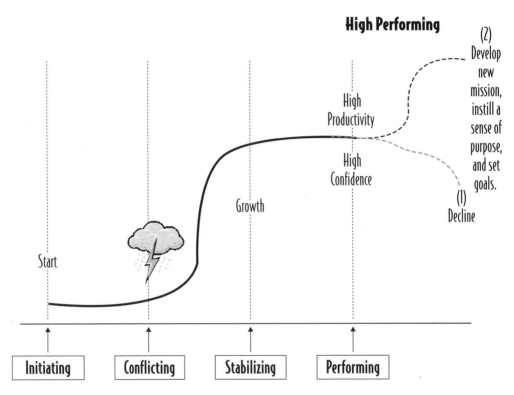

**Figure 2.4.**   Stages of High-Performing Teams

# Life Cycles of the Stages

The duration and intensity of each of the stages varies from one team to the next. A number of factors can affect the length of time it takes to progress through the stages, including available resources, complexity of the task, organization support, member readiness, leadership competency, and the leader's ability to adapt his or her style in a manner that meets the needs of the situation. It may take considerable time for one team to reach the Performing stage, while another team is at the Performing stage within a short period. Some groups never reach the Performing stage.

While the obvious goal is to reach the Performing stage as soon as possible, it is a futile exercise to attempt to skip or rush through stages in the development of the team. Research indicates that those groups that try may carry out their tasks, but do not produce optimum performance and their members are dissatisfied with the process or output.

Knowing that it is normal for a team to go through these stages will help your team understand and anticipate the process and take action to build more productive relationships and performance.

"The teaming process has been compared to a roller coaster ride."

*Kahn, Kroeber, and Kingsury, 1974*

Progress may often go from climbing to stalling to falling. Feelings may move from excited as the project begins to anxious or impatient as team members realize the extent of the undertaking, to encouraged as useful information is gathered, to frustrated as the team meets roadblocks and has to devise new or revised plans, to confident with a sense of accomplishment as the team reaches new heights in performance.

# Summary of the Concepts and Principles

Below is a summary of the Stages of Team Performance for ease of review in the future.

**Teams are today's reality.**
Teams benefit both organizations and individuals. Today, organizations find teams to be a necessary component in planning their future, generating creative ideas, solving problems, raising performance levels, and implementing business strategies.

**Teams provide growth opportunities.**
Being part of a team provides individuals an opportunity to widen their experience, deepen knowledge, and master skills in ways that might not be available to them as individual contributors.

**Teams progress through unique stages of development.**
Theory on team development indicates that teams, like individuals, progress through predictable stages over time. We call these stages Initiating, Conflicting, Stabilizing, and Performing.

**Team performance is two-dimensional.**
There are two dimensions of team performance: Task and Relationship. Each stage has its unique interpersonal challenges that must be understood and addressed, as well as specific tasks to be accomplished, before the group can progress to the next stage.

**Team goals must align with organizational goals.**
To be effective, team goals must be measurable and aligned with the overall organizational goals and objectives.

**Team progress can be affected by the team's characteristics.**
The progression of team development is not always sequential. Teams rotate through the stages repeatedly, depending on the team's characteristics. A successful team is one that can skillfully move among these stages as situations shift.

**Team development is essential to success.**
Teams can stagger and stop at any stage. Failure to pay attention to the important development steps at any one stage may cause the team to relapse to that stage.

**Teams experience highs and lows.**
Understanding the four performance stages will help your team recognize the predictable and inevitable highs and lows that are a part of a team's development. Applying the action steps will help your team overcome barriers and move the team forward.

**Team success is driven by individual effort and collective contributions.**
For teams to maximize their performance requires that each individual team member makes a concerted effort to grow in both relationship and task aspects.

**Team building is continuous.**
Team building is more than a one-time event; it is an ongoing process that involves hard work and determination.

**Teaming is both a destination and a journey.**
While the destination is the goal, there is value in the journey and it can be a rewarding experience.

# Our Team

## Perception of Team's Stage

When the workshop facilitator provides the results of the TPI assessment your team took, enter the scores in the appropriate stage below.

| Initiating | Conflicting | Stabilizing | Performing |
|---|---|---|---|
|  |  |  |  |

## Perception of Team Leader's Style

Enter the perception your team members had of your leader's style scores in the appropriate box below.

| Directing | Coaching | Facilitating | Delegating |
|---|---|---|---|
|  |  |  |  |

# III

# Individual and Team Development Plans

Individual Development Plan
Team Development Plan

# Individual Development Plan

The check sheets and the worksheets that follow are provided to help you select the exercises that you can use to develop your skills as a team member on your own.

**Instructions**

1. Transfer the information you checked in the Characteristics of the Four Stages of Team Performance section of the last chapter (page 39) under the heading Members' Roles to the Individual Development Plan Check Sheet on the next page.

2. Review the list of checked items and select *two* areas that you would most like to develop and improve on. Complete an Individual Development Action Plan Worksheet for each of the two areas.

3. Next, select an exercise from the next section of your workbook that you believe will help you in your desire to be a better team member. Each exercise in Part IV of this workbook includes an overview, situational content, instructions for completing the exercise, and any applicable worksheets. Each has been designed to be completed in one to two hours. They are listed below, categorized by area of interest. Other ideas are listed in Part V of this workbook by stage of development.

# Individual Development Plan Check Sheet

**Initiating Stage (Members' Roles, page 18)**

❑ Asking questions to clarify team's initial purpose and tasks

❑ Having patience with the process

❑ Listening actively

❑ Being open to new ideas

❑ Resisting pre-judgments and preconceived attitudes

**Conflicting Stage (Members' Roles, pages 22–23)**

❑ Seeking clarity about purpose, roles, and responsibilities

❑ Risking self-disclosure

❑ Initiating ideas

❑ Respecting diversity of team members

❑ Accepting that conflict is inevitable and finding ways to use it effectively

❑ Speaking only for yourself

❑ Helping the team reach consensus on purpose, goals, and roles

**Stabilizing Stage (Members' Roles, page 26)**

❑ Preparing for and contributing during team meetings

❑ Voicing both opposing and confirming viewpoints

❑ Buying into objectives and activities

❑ Communicating, communicating, and communicating

❑ Requesting and accepting feedback

❑ Self-reinforcing team ground rules

❑ Committing to a "no surprises" contract with other team members

❑ Working proactively for the benefit of the team

❑ Demonstrating active listening and a willingness to change

❑ Building trust by honoring commitments

❑ Taking responsibility for a professional development plan with stretch goals that align with the team's goals and the organization's strategy

**Performing Stage (Members' Roles, pages 30–31)**

❑ Having a sense of individual responsibility for the team's success

❑ Deferring to team needs; keeping team objectives in the forefront while managing your personal precedence

❑ Introducing and cultivating new ideas

- ❑ Committing to mutual accountability
- ❑ Applying positive pressure to assure the team achieves effective and satisfying results
- ❑ Taking full responsibility for tasks and relationships
- ❑ Eliminating duplication of efforts by acknowledging and using each member's unique contributions to the team's objective
- ❑ Keeping up with the latest trends and developments in your field and industry
- ❑ Presenting the team's mission, goals, plans, and purpose energetically to others outside the team

# Individual Development Action Plan Worksheet

| Action Plan | Start Date | Milestone Dates | Completion Date |
|---|---|---|---|
| Action Area: | | | |

| Why I chose this area: |
|---|
| |

| What are my expectations for improvement? |
|---|
| |

| What resources will I need? |
|---|
| |

| How will I use it? To what extent will it make me a better employee? Benefit the team? The organization? |
|---|
| |

| What potential roadblocks might get in the way? How will I overcome them? |
|---|
| |

| How will I know I am successful? How will my team know? My organization? |
|---|
| |

# Individual Development Action Plan Worksheet

| Action Plan | Start Date | Milestone Dates | Completion Date |
|---|---|---|---|
| Action Area: | | | |

**Why I chose this area:**

**What are my expectations for improvement?**

**What resources will I need?**

**How will I use it? To what extent will it make me a better employee? Benefit the team? The organization?**

**What potential roadblocks might get in the way? How will I overcome them?**

**How will I know I am successful? How will my team know? My organization?**

# Team Development Plan

You will use this activity to determine the development activities appropriate for your team after this workshop.

### Instructions

1. Transfer the information you checked in the Characteristics of the Four Stages of Team Performance section under the heading Action Steps to Be Accomplished to the following Team Development Plan Check Sheet.

2. Choose the top three areas of development you feel are the most important to your team's success and rank order them.

# Team Development Plan Check Sheet

Use the left section of the check box to transfer the information you checked as Action Steps, and use the right section of the box to indicate the rank order of your top three areas for team development.

### Initiating Stage (Action Steps to Be Accomplished, page 19)

- [ ] Building a common purpose
- [ ] Identifying interests and values
- [ ] Assessing talent resources (*who* has *what* to contribute).
- [ ] Determining stakeholders' and clients/customers' expectations
- [ ] Developing goals that are aligned with the organization's strategic intent
- [ ] Discussing individual and team expectations
- [ ] Sharing relevant information
- [ ] Encouraging interactive dialogue
- [ ] Providing structure and direction to team issues
- [ ] Engaging in team activities that build trust and open communication

### Conflicting Stage (Action Steps to Be Accomplished, page 23)

- [ ] Ensuring conflicting stage issues are addressed
- [ ] Encouraging an open flow of communication
- [ ] Supporting collaborative team efforts
- [ ] Involving everyone in the discussion; inquiring into differences
- [ ] Clarifying roles and responsibilities
- [ ] Discussing individual and mutual accountability
- [ ] Establishing and building ground rules(rules of behavior—what is and what is not appropriate)
- [ ] Discussing and concurring on how you will disagree
- [ ] Learning to address topics that are potentially embarrassing or threatening
- [ ] Discussing and agreeing on a decision-making process
- [ ] Defining a rewards and recognition structure

### Stabilizing Stage (Action Steps to Be Accomplished, pages 26–27)

- [ ] Talking openly about issues and concerns
- [ ] Giving positive and constructive feedback
- [ ] Developing processes for information sharing, feedback, and resource allocation
- [ ] Having open forums on tasks and relationships, both internal and external; negotiating where appropriate

☑ Building on positive behaviors and changing unsupportive behaviors

☑ Supporting consensus decision-making efforts

☑ Assuring that team goals are clear, specific, and measurable and that all team members accept the goals and their roles in achieving them

☑ Performing roles and responsibilities with proficiency

☑ Setting high expectations and developing the skills and knowledge required to help the team do what it says it will do

## Performing Stage (Action Steps to Be Accomplished, page 31)

☑ Focusing on the big picture and pragmatic deliverables and solutions

☑ Bringing ideas to reality

☑ Evaluating processes and procedures to determine potential areas for improvement

☑ Communicating views and feelings

☑ Delegating freely within the team

☑ Continuously raising the bar

☑ Setting fresh and challenging goals

☑ Packaging our success factors as a repeatable process

# IV

# Exercises for Developing and Increasing Individual and Team Performance

# Introduction

This part of your workbook consists of selected exercises with accompanying worksheets for self- and team development. They have been designed to be completed independently, in small groups, or within a team-building workshop. Two or more can work together on common development activities and exercises or within a coach/mentor relationship, or team leaders can select specific exercises for team development. Your workshop facilitator may also wish to incorporate some of the following exercises in conjunction with the exercises in the Facilitator's Guide.

Each exercise includes an overview, the situational content, and any necessary worksheets. They have been designed to be completed in one to two hours. See the chart below to choose the exercises that are best for your purposes.

| | Exercise | Development Area | Focus Interpersonal | Task | Page |
|---|---|---|---|---|---|
| 1. | What's Important to Me, What's Important to You? | Intra-Member Knowledge | ✓ | | 56 |
| 2. | Trust Me, Trust You | Trust | ✓ | | 63 |
| 3. | Speak Up, Listen Up | Communication | ✓ | | 67 |
| 4. | Think "We" Rather Than "I Versus You" | Conflict | ✓ | | 75 |
| 5. | Giving and Receiving Feedback | Feedback | ✓ | | 80 |
| 6. | Career Development Journal | Career Development | ✓ | ✓ | 86 |
| 7. | Individual Success Versus Team Success | Team Player | ✓ | ✓ | 88 |
| 8. | Stylemarks of High-Performing Teams | Team Performance | ✓ | ✓ | 91 |
| 9. | Plan of Action and Milestone (POA&M) | Action Planning | ✓ | ✓ | 95 |

# Exercise 1. What's Important to Me, What's Important to You?

How well do your team members know you? Do they know what is important to you? Your values, your strengths, your motivators? And do you know what is important to the other members of your team?

When a team is newly formed, an essential first step is for members to become acquainted. The information gained will lay critical groundwork for the work the team will be doing and how the members will work together.

Even when team members have been together for a while and think they know "everything there is to know" about each other, it is good to dedicate time to become reacquainted. A getting-acquainted activity provides members an opportunity to challenge assumptions and change previous impressions. This can also be important when a new member joins the team.

When asked what they want, employees will typically say something like, "I want my team to know me as an individual (interests, values, competencies, and motivators) and support me in meeting my needs." Yet, unless we do so though an organized exercise, many of us are reticent to broach our needs and assert our talents.

Use the exercise on the following pages to gather information about your team. Once you know what's important to your co-workers and the talents they bring to the team, you will be able to offer support that better fits their needs. This exercise can be divided into two or three sessions, with members answering some of the questions as pre-work.

This exercise provides an opportunity for you to acknowledge what is important to you, the unique combination of interests, values, skills, and talents you bring to the team, and what you need from your team members to be successful. You will learn more about your colleagues' values, satisfiers, strengths, and ways you can support them. The exercise will also set the stage for a discussion of team values and an inventory of your team's talent.

1.  Begin by answering the five questions in the What's Important to Me Worksheet on page 58.

2.  Next, pair with an associate who will:

    o   Listen to your answers and ask clarifying questions.

    o   Add information to your list that she or he has discerned but you have not thought of yourself.

    o   Ask probing questions so that the two of you together can come up with additional items to add.

3.  Switch roles with your partner and repeat Item 2. When interviewing your partner, use the Co-Worker's Profile Worksheet on page 60 to record your notes.

4.  Introduce your partner to the other team members using what you have learned.

5.  Keep notes during your co-workers' introductions.

## What's Important to Me Worksheet

1. What interests you? Of all the waking hours you spend on the job, what time do you enjoy most?

    Define your interests in terms of career activities.

2. What are your values? Like most people, you spend considerable time in the workplace. What kind of working environment is worth so much of your valuable talent and time?

    List three values that are important at this time in your career/life.

    A

    B

    C

3. Think about the talents (key competencies, skills, knowledge, and attitude) you bring to this team and answer the questions below.

    Describe what you do well (include any "hidden talents" that everyone on the team may not know about).

    Give examples of how you use (or could use) these talents to contribute to the team's success.

4. What specific support do you need? Complete this sentence: The specific support I need from this team to be successful is

5. Understanding that people differ in the way they like to be recognized and want to be rewarded . . .

How do you preferred to be recognized? (✓) ❏ Publicly ❏ Privately ❏ Other

For what would you like to be recognized?

In what form would you like to be rewarded?

Give an example of a recognition that was particularly meaningful to you and what made it special.

## Co-Worker's Profile Worksheet

Record your notes from your co-worker's What's Important to Me answers below.

   Name:

1. His or her interests are

2. His or her values are

3. Key talents (competencies, skills, knowledge, and attitude) she or he brings to the team and how he or she contributes to the team's success:

   Key talents:

   Contributions:

4. Specific support he or she needs from the team to be successful:

5. How he or she likes to be recognized:

## Team and Personal Values Worksheet

It is essential for a team to clarify its values and determine how each member's values connect to the team's values. One way to determine this linkage is through a discussion of what values are important to each individual team member and what values are essential to the team's success.

The goal is for members to clarify together which values are central to their shared work. When team members collaborate on what is most important to them, a shared commitment can emerge.

### Team Values

Here are some questions to consider when creating a charter of team values. If your team has already developed team value statements, now is a good time to revisit your values and evaluate how well you are living them.

- What do we stand for?
- How do we treat our customers (both internal and external)?
- Which values do we need to develop, or which are expressed but neglected?
- How do we want to treat each other at work?
- How do we want to be seen by others (internally and externally)?
- What team member attitudes and behaviors do we want to recognize and reward?
- How do our team values link to the organization's values?

### Personal Values

Using your response to number 2 on the What's Important to Me Worksheet as a reference, answer the following questions.

Do your values link to the team's values?

If so, how? If not, why do you think there is a mismatch?

# Talent Inventory Discussion Worksheet

Thinking of your team as a whole, complete and discuss the questions below using the information gained so far while doing this exercise.

What does the What's Important to Me exercise tell us about how well we know our fellow team members? Check (✓) the appropriate response.

❐ We really don't know each other very well.

❐ There is much more we can learn about each other.

❐ We know each other quite well.

To what extent is the talent on this team being utilized?

❐ Highly underutilized

❐ Underutilized

❐ Utilized

❐ Highly utilized

Explain your answer.

Circle the number on the continuum below that most characterizes your team's skills, knowledge, and attitudes.

**Skills and Knowledge**

| Lack of task skills impedes our team's performance | | | Strong task skills enhance our team's performance | |
|---|---|---|---|---|
| 1 | 2 | 3 | 4 | 5 |

| Lack of interpersonal skills hinders our team's performance | | | Strong interpersonal skills augment our team's performance | |
|---|---|---|---|---|
| 1 | 2 | 3 | 4 | 5 |

**Attitudes**

| Negative attitudes | | | | Positive attitudes |
|---|---|---|---|---|
| 1 | 2 | 3 | 4 | 5 |

Explain your choices.

How well do we support our team members?

❐ Rarely          ❐ Occasionally          ❐ Generally          ❐ Continually

How and where can we be more supportive?

# Exercise 2. Trust Me, Trust You

Trust within a team begins with a common understanding of expectations and mutual goals, roles and outcomes. It is activated with the belief that every member is capable of performing roles and responsibilities with proficiency and intends to give his or her best effort to accomplish the goals of a team.

Let's be clear. Trust takes hard work and time to grow, develop, and maintain. Team members, while sharing a series of common experiences, must learn to understand and accept each other and act in a manner that is team-serving rather than self-serving. However, the hard work is worth the effort to build an environment of trust. Trust forms the foundation for understanding, effective communication, openness, commitment, involvement, and high performance.

Scholtes (1998, p. 3) maintains that, "Trust requires the coexistence of two converging beliefs. When I believe you are competent and that you care about me, I will trust you. Competency alone or caring by itself will not engender trust. Both are necessary."

Use the Trust Assessment Worksheet on the next page to help you evaluate the level of trust on your team and determine changes that both you and the team might take to improve trust.

> ## Trust
>
> To have belief or confidence in the purpose, honesty, actions, competency, and intent of a person, organization, or team based on predictable behaviors observed over time.

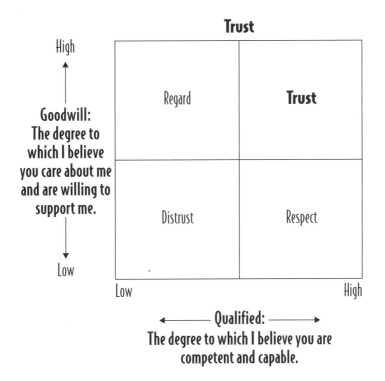

Scholtes, Paul R. *The Leader's Handbook.* The McGraw-Hill Companies. Used with permission.

## Trust Assessment Worksheet

What is the level of trust on your team?

❒ Very little trust

❒ Guarded and cautionary trust

❒ Oscillating and vacillating trust

❒ Open and complete trust

On the next page is a list of personal characteristics and behaviors that foster and create trust on a team. As you read the characteristics, check the ones that you think those on your team do well. Then total your check marks and answer the questions below.

**Total "Does Well" Score:** _____

1. Pick one or two characteristics that you checked and describe how they are demonstrated on your team.

2. Of the characteristics you did not check, which one or two behaviors and attitudes could your team change that would improve team trust?

3. What actions could you personally take that would help to build or restore trust on your team?

## Trust Characteristics

This is shown in the figure below.

- ❏ **Competency.** Performs roles and responsibilities with proficiency. Sets high expectations and develops the skills and knowledge required to help the team do what it says it will do.

- ❏ **Truthfulness and Vulnerability.** Is real and honest with one's self and others. No withholding or giving misleading information. No spreading rumors or talking behind people's backs. Admits mistakes and apologizes.

- ❏ **Creditability and Consistency.** Walks the talk. Provides accurate communication and keeps others up-to-date with good news and bad. Is unfailing and logical.

- ❏ **Accountability and Reliability.** Holds one's self and others accountable for their work. Can be counted on to meet deadlines, adhere to rules and performance standards. Takes ownership at both individual and team levels. When agrees to do something, does it.

- ❏ **Connectivity.** Understands and appreciates co-workers' personalities, values, interests, cultural differences, goals, weaknesses, and strengths. Finds ways to affirm others' uniqueness.

- ❏ **Loyalty and Support.** Willingly provides backup to other team members to assure quality work and that deadlines are met. Encourages and supports appropriate risk taking. Pledges that disputes will remain within the team, and once a decision or conclusion is made or reached, leaves as a team, "speaks with one voice," and abides by the conclusions.

❐ **Inclusion.** Shares knowledge and information. Is warm and accepting versus remote and rejecting. Includes others in team discussion, problem solving, and decision making. Respects opposing and counterpoising views.

❐ **Feedback.** Gives and receives feedback for the benefit of the team. Communicates needs, attitudes, and feelings, even about the other person. Describes behaviors. Clarifies meanings and expectations. Expresses thoughts and feelings without defensiveness.

❐ **Commitment.** Invests the emotional and cognitive energy and effort required to improve performance and working relationships.

# Exercise 3. Speak Up, Listen Up

Good communication is critical to effective teamwork. Many of the problems that occur within a team can be the result of faulty communication.

Lack of communication skills not only has a destructive effect on the team, but may also impede your personal success in the workplace.

According to a report published by the National Association of Colleges and Employers

> **Communication**
>
> A process by which information is exchanged between people by means of speaking, writing, or using a common system of symbols, signs, or behaviors.

(NACE), employers say they consider communication skills to be important in job candidates, but find that many potential employees lack them. When asked about "soft" skills, qualities, and characteristics in job candidates, employers responding to NACE's Job Outlook report (NACE, 2006) cited communication skills as most important. At the same time, however, when asked about candidate "holes," most identified communication skills. Marilyn Mackes, NACE executive director said:

> "For more than ten years, we've asked employers about key skills, and they have consistently named communication skills as critical, yet have also said this is something many candidates lack.
>
> "We've found that employers look for candidates who can bring with them skills that will enable them to succeed in the workplace. Communication and teamwork skills, flexibility, a strong work ethic, honesty and integrity, interpersonal skills—all of those things help the candidate work effectively.
>
> "Research leads to the conclusion that there is a positive correlation between effective communication and each of the following factors: productivity, personal satisfaction, rewarding relationships and effective problem solving" (p. 109)

With such strong evidence that there is a significant payoff for effective communications in the workplace, doesn't it make sense to devote some time and effort to developing your one-on-one and team communication skills?

The NACE report continues: "Clarity of communication is influenced by the extent that those who are sending and those who are listening are aware of their communication skills." Some people presume they communicate clearly and are surprised when the message they intended is misread or misunderstood by the receiver. An accurate assessment of your communication skills is important. How can you fix something unless you know what is broken? The reality is that, when it comes to communication, there is room for improvement for everyone.

Since giving and receiving information is the lifeblood of effective team performance, it is important that team members understand the communication process and

## Communication Components

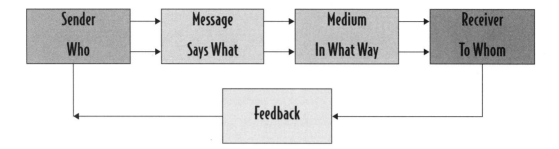

the factors that influence effective communications. The figure above provides an overview of the communication process and points out each of the following communication components:

- Sender
- Message
- Medium
- Receiver
- Feedback

Communication is a two-way process that involves both sending and receiving messages. Clear communication is the responsibility of both the sender and the receiver.

Understanding the process will give you insight into your own communication strengths and weaknesses. As you review the different forms of communication below, identify areas that may require your special attention.

### Face-to-Face Communication

Face-to-face is the most efficient form of communication because participants benefit both from the meaning of the words, as well as from the interpretation carried by body language and the voice aspects supplementing the verbal message. A recent Harvard/Columbia study showed a 38 percent increase in retention with face-to-face meetings (Hayward, 2004). Face-to-face is desirable for new relationships, renewing old relationships, communicating sensitive information or bad news and for resolving conflicts. For virtual teams, face-to-face communication is limited or non-existent and it is all the more important that they are skilled in other forms of communication.

**Words, Body Language, and Tone of Voice**   In his studies, Albert Mehrabian (1981) concluded there are three elements to face-to-face communication. He said

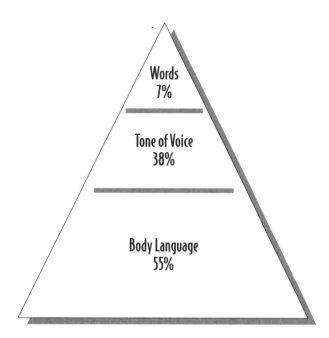

that 55 percent of what we learn from others comes from their nonverbal communications, 38 percent comes from the tone of their voice, and 7 percent comes from the words they say. This is shown in the figure above.

***Words***   It is a mistake to discount the value of words, even though they are credited with only 7 percent of what we learn from others. To make your content more meaningful:

- Give relevant information

- Organize your ideas

- Choose the right words

- Know and cover the receiver's concerns (facts and details, possibilities and options, pros, cons, and impact on people).

***Body Language***   Actions speak louder than words. People believe what they see more than what they hear. Body language is a constant, nonverbal flow of communication. Body language is transmitted through the eyes, face, hands, arms, legs, and posture. Without saying anything (and sometimes without realizing it), your body language can reveal what you are feeling and thinking. For example, without exchanging a word, you can guess what a co-worker is feeling and thinking when she rolls her eyes in exasperation when you return to her desk (again) to say you could not find the Brecken file . . . and could she please help you find it? Do you know what nonverbal messages you are sending? Have you taken an inventory recently? If you are unsure of your nonverbal strengths and weaknesses, ask for feedback from those who know you.

**Eye contact** is one of the most powerful of all the body language skills. Good eye contact projects self-confidence and professionalism. It lets others know that you are interested, receptive, and attentive to what they are saying. Eye contact allows you to listen to others' feelings, as well as to their words.

Your **facial expression** is like a commercial that lets everyone around you know whether you are happy, sad, excited, or angry. Be careful not to let the stresses of the day gather on your forehead. Smiling is a universal language that tends to relax and bond people when used at appropriate times. While many people feel that a stoic, dead-pan look expresses professionalism, it is often interpreted as being over-controlling, boring, rigid, inflexible, or unfriendly.

**Body posture and movement** show your energy level and interest in what others are saying. Body position can be used to indicate interest by leaning forward. Disinterest or thought about what's been said can be indicated by leaning backward. Too much leaning backward might indicate an arrogance or aloofness.

**Hand and arm gestures** that are excessive or inappropriate can be distracting and attract attention; subtle movements can be used to strengthen key points (e.g., two thumbs up to illustrate strong endorsement; connecting the index finger and the thumb forming a circle to indicate OK; or pointing the index finger up while saying, "This is our number one priority"). However, playing with objects (pencils, rings, hair, tie, etc.) as you speak with someone may be interpreted as impatience or disinterest.

*Tone of Voice*

**Pace.** Are you a fast talker or do you go at a slow and easy pace? By pacing another's rate of speech, you can close the communication gap and have more success in your communication. Is there a lot of intensity and excitement in your voice, or do you usually sound calm and relaxed? The tone you use may communicate what you think or feel. For example, an abrupt speed and very loud tone may be interpreted as, "I'm in control and not open to your point of view!" A monotone and flat voice may say, "I'm bored or disinterested." A high-pitched and emphatic voice conveys enthusiasm.

How interesting is your vocal expression? Do you know? Take the mini quiz below by checking the phrases you think describe you. Next, ask your co-workers for feedback on your vocal expression.

❏ Are you warm and friendly?

❏ Or are you business-focused and formal?

❏ Do you speak too loudly?

❏ Or do you speak so softly that is difficult to hear what you are saying?

## Telephone Communication

When talking on the telephone, body language disappears and 86 percent of the message is communicated by tone of voice (see the figure).

Below are five tips you can use to improve your telephone communication skills.

1. Ask several people to give you feedback about your telephone communication style (including speakerphone).

2. During any conversation, encourage the listener to ask questions.

3. Smile when talking.

4. Breathe (deep, long, and slow).

5. Facilitate good chemistry by tailoring your style to the individual with whom you are talking. If he or she is speaking with a no-nonsense, abrupt style, emulate his or her direct approach. If he or she appears detached and serious, limit your small talk.

## Congruent Communication

To be effective in your communication, it is important that what you say (verbal) matches how you act (nonverbal, visual) and the way you say it (vocal). This is achieved when verbal (words), nonverbal communication (eyes, face, hands, arms, legs, and posture), and voice (expression, volume, tone, and pace) convey the same message. Communication specialists call this communication congruency. This congruency communicates your honesty and commitment.

## Tips for the Receiver

If you are like many people, you may not have given much thought to your role as a receiver in the communication process. Yet, if you accept that successful communication is a two-way process, doesn't it make sense to understand the factors that influence how other members of a team take in information, interpret and evaluate messages?

In an interesting study of team success and failure, Hirokawa, DeGooyer, and Valde (2003) reported that "Poor listening, close-minded interaction among team members, and the absence of proper information flow among team members was especially problematic for team success" (p. 154).

Knowing how communication can be distorted and misunderstood is a good place to start. The figure below illustrates how communication is filtered. As you review the tips below, you may be surprised to find how your attitude, feelings, and perceptions can affect how you receive the sender's message and what you can do to improve your communication receiver skills.

- **Be aware of your feelings toward the speaker and the message.** There may be a situation in which you don't particularly care for the speaker or topic, but don't let your feelings keep you from hearing what is being said.

- **Don't disregard the message because of a negative past experience.** The speaker's idea was tried before without success, so you refuse to evaluate the information objectively. If you are constantly saying (or thinking), "We've already tried this" or "It can't be done," you may be seen as a cynic with a negative attitude.

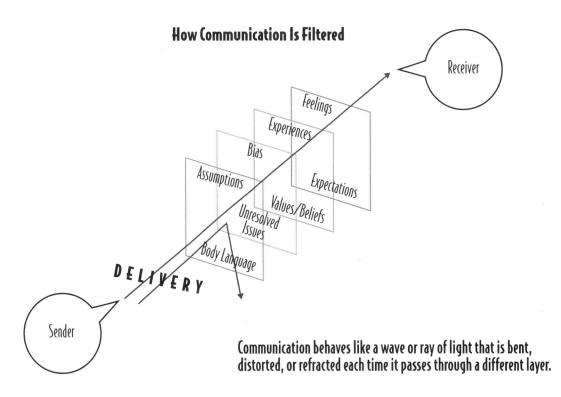

## How Communication Is Filtered

Communication behaves like a wave or ray of light that is bent, distorted, or refracted each time it passes through a different layer.

- **Check for hidden agendas.** If you are in competition with the speaker, you may hear only what meets your own needs and reject or sabotage the overall intent of the sender's message.

- **Avoid preconceptions and expectations.** By assuming because the speaker is younger, older, holds a lower position, is of a different ethic group, etc., or you think she or he doesn't deserve your attention, you are devaluing the speaker and may be dismissing an excellent proposal from someone with a fresh perspective.

- **Become an active listener.** Has anyone ever accused you of not listening? A co-worker or family member may have said, "You are not listening to me. I can tell by your expression you haven't hear a word I've said" or perhaps you have been in a situation in which the other person took telephone calls or tapped his or her pencil impatiently when you were attempting to present an idea or position. Remember how you felt? These are common examples of poor listening.

  Active listening is as important to communication as effective sending. Carl Rogers contends that "Active listening is an important way to bring about changes in people . . . clinical and research evidence clearly shows that sensitive listening is a most effective agent for individual personality change and group development" (Rogers & Farson, 1987, p. 1). If your listening skills need improvement, you are not alone. Gregory Huszczo maintains, "It appears that most adults in the world of work are terrible listeners. We feel so busy that we don't have the patience to listen. We want to get our point across, so we sell our ideas rather than attend to what the other person is saying. You must show respect in order to have positive impact on relationships. The basic way we show respect to others is by listening to them"(Huszczo, 1996, p. 133).

  The assessment on the following page is designed to help you reflect upon your listening skills and identify and adopt specific tips that will make you a better listener.

- **Give feedback.** As the receiver, it is your responsibility to let the sender know your understanding of what he or she is communicating. Your feedback can be verbal or nonverbal. For example, nodding your head and saying, "You make a convincing case for selecting the ABC software. I appreciate the thoroughness of your presentation." Even more critical is feedback that lets the sender know that his or her message needs to be clarified. You can do this by saying, "Let me be sure I understand what you are proposing" or "Did I hear you correctly? You are suggesting that . . . ?"

## Active Listening Assessment

Review the active listening tips below. As you read, check those tips you could do better. Then choose and commit to two tips that you are willing to act on to improve your listening skills. List the tips you chose below:

1. _____

2. _____

**Tips on Being a Good Listener**

❐ Commit to listen objectively and openly.

❐ Acknowledge the speaker. Be attentive and show you are being attentive. By nodding occasionally as someone speaks, you can indicate acknowledgement, approval, or agreement with what is being said.

❐ Listen for content, meaning, and feeling. Describe what you hear by rephrasing in your own words or asking questions about specific points to be sure you received the message accurately.

❐ Try not to interrupt.

❐ Avoid changing the subject too quickly. This action suggests you are not interested in what the other person has to say.

❐ Pay attention to body language (yours and the other person's).

❐ Become comfortable with silence. Some people think aloud, while others need time to think before they respond.

❐ Avoid telling others how they should or shouldn't feel. Feelings are neither right nor wrong.

❐ Don't disregard the message because of your feelings toward the speaker and/or the message.

❐ Be patient with others' communication styles (volume, expression, tone, and pace) and try to match your style to theirs.

❐ Practice. Learning to be a good listener is no easy task. It takes time and concentration, but it enhances your personal and professional effectiveness and it is well worth the effort.

# Exercise 4. Think "We" Rather Than "I Versus You"

Conflict is an inevitable reality. Conflict occurs when an individual's or team's needs and values infringe on the needs and concerns of others.

Conflict develops because we are dealing with people's tasks, pride, self-image, values, and sense of mission or purpose.

Causes of conflict stem from a variety of factors: inadequate conflict management skills; differences in communication styles; disagreements about work assignments, agendas, and priorities; incorrect, misleading, or insufficient information; lack of openness and truthfulness; and unclear roles and responsibilities.

Conflict can be healthy if it is handled and resolved constructively. If managed poorly, it can be destructive not only interpersonally but for the team as well.

Conflict is constructive when it:

- Opens up and clarifies issues

- Generates creative ideas

- Brings a variety of views

- Helps resolve problems and gain closure

- Minimizes failure

Conflict is destructive when it:

- Increases levels of mistrust

- Advances loss of emotional control

- Diminishes logic and rationale

- Polarizes people and the team

- Injures reputation (individual or team)

- Interrupts productivity

- Damages morale and increases stress

## Conflict

An active disagreement or clash between people with opposing opinions, ideas, or principles.

"It does not matter how creatively we deny responsibility for the effectiveness of our communications and the resolution of our conflicts. None of our conflicts could have happened without our active or passive participation." (Cloke & Goldsmith, 2000, p. 142)

When all members of the team are thinking alike, no one is really thinking. Out of disagreement or conflict often comes a new understanding or interpretation of an issue that would not have otherwise been possible.

"While it takes time to resolve disputes, it also takes time not to resolve them. If we count up the time and money we spend on unresolved conflicts, it is nearly always far in excess of the time and money it would take to sit and work out solutions." (Cloke & Goldsmith, 2000, p. 10)

## What is your approach to conflict?

Check the statements below that are characteristic of you:

- ❐ Do you tend to take an aggressive "do whatever it takes" to get what you think must be done, even if it may harm a relationship?

- ❐ Do you find conflict upsetting and avoid it as long as possible?

- ❐ Do you acknowledge the potential conflict but smooth it over because you don't want to say something you may regret and harm the relationship?

- ❐ Do you take a "let's meet in the middle" approach to get things settled and let both parties come away with something?

None of the above approaches is wrong. Each can be effective depending on the situation, but each has its shortcomings. For example, if your preferred way of dealing with conflict is to ignore it, hoping it will melt away, chances are that it will not disappear but grow bigger. When you aggressively push through an idea without buy-in from others, you may come to an expedient decision but fail to obtain the needed support for implementation. When your desire is to accommodate others, the results may be a watered-down solution that is not useful. People tend to over-rely on a particular approach and may neglect another way that could be more productive.

## Power

Power is often used to settle differences. The power may come from various sources, as shown in the figure below.

When power is used constructively (that is, through persuasive arguments based on reason and negotiation), members will mobilize and pull together. Positive power dynamics can increase interdependence and synergy.

Power misused and abused consistently leads to winners and losers, with losers directly or indirectly failing to support the initiative.

**Sources of Power**

## Collaboration

Collaboration is another, but challenging approach to conflict management. Collaboration is also referred to as negotiation, or integration.

> **Collaboration**
>
> Coaction. To work jointly with others or together for a special purpose.

Teams often collaborate closely in order to reach consensus or agreement. The ability to use collaboration requires the recognition of and respect for everyone's ideas, opinions, and suggestions.

Not every point will meet everyone's complete approval. Everyone being of one mind is not the goal. The goal is to have individuals accept a point of view based on logic. When individuals can understand and accept the logic or a differing point of view, you can assume you have reached consensus.

Collaboration is effective because it

- Encourages learning
- Builds commitment to agreed decisions
- Decreases stress
- Builds cohesiveness
- Improves relationships and teamwork
- Takes a proactive approach and is more long-term

Collaboration is challenging because it:

- Takes time
- Takes planning
- Necessitates a learning curve
- Requires vulnerability
- Takes action
- Requires commitment

## Tips and Guidelines for Managing Conflict

A key dynamic of managing conflict is discussion among members. Discussions are ways to share information, to debate issues, and to make decisions. Yet, too often, discussion can turn into a war of words rather than a tool for achieving goals. When this happens, some team members may try to dominate, while others tend to withdraw. To ensure that discussions are productive, your team needs to establish some basic guidelines (that is, conflict management ground rules) for how members interact. Here are typical examples:

| | |
|---|---|
| Meet conflict head-on | Check your ego at the door |
| Assume positive intent | Avoid "win-lose" statements |
| Keep conflicts within the team | Ask questions for understanding |
| Question your own reactions | No hidden agendas |
| Use "I" statements and speak | Only for yourself |
| Don't get other team members involved in the discussion who are not part of the conflict | Agree to disagree—understand hat healthy disagreements will build better decisions |
| No personal attacks; focus on issues and behaviors, not personalities | Avoid changing minds in order to evade conflict and to achieve harmony |

**Define the problem.** Be specific in describing the situation. Answer the who, what, where, how, and when questions, the impact of behaviors on stakeholders, decisions, processes, and outcomes.

**Generate potential solutions.** Brainstorm prospective solutions, then reality check them by evaluating pros and cons, and cause and effect of each solution.

**Question the initial agreement.** Explore the reasons underlying apparent agreements and make sure that members have willingly agreed.

**Reach agreement.** Elicit and check out solutions until parties agree on a common course of action. When at an impasse, bring in an objective third party.

**Plan implementation of the solution.** Determine the how and when. Include a time and date to reevaluate the solution. Understanding conflict and practicing the different methods and strategies for managing it will result in better teamwork, improved productivity, and more creative solutions.

Now let's take a look at how you manage conflict. The Conflict Management Worksheet on the following page will help you recognize how you manage conflict. Draw from the Tips and Guidelines for Managing Conflict you just read to help you determine what you could do to improve your conflict resolution skills.

## Conflict Management Worksheet

Think about how you manage conflict. Complete the sentence stem by checking your usual method for dealing with conflict.

Generally I deal with conflict by . . .

❐ Letting one or a few aggressively push a view through without my input

❐ Ignoring it, hoping it will resolve itself

❐ Trying to patch it over, only to see it reemerge

❐ Collaborating, encouraging, and accepting differing points of view

Next, write your answers to the following questions and then discuss your answers with your team members.

1. What are your feelings, thoughts, and concerns when you are engaged in conflict?

2. How do you contribute to conflict?

3. List three things you could do to improve your conflict resolution skills.

    A.

    B.

    C.

# Exercise 5. Giving and Receiving Feedback

Feedback is an essential component to interpersonal and team effectiveness, as it helps the communicators and the recipients to understand the effects of their behavior.

Most people do not see themselves as others see them, and they are often unaware of the impact their actions have on others. Feedback is essential to learning. If people don't fully appreciate their strengths, how can they use them to their advantage? If they never find out how their actions create problems for others, how will they know what to change? And if they never understand the impact they have, why would they want to make a concerted effort to improve?

Generally, people value constructive feedback. They find that feedback adds an important dimension to their personal relationships and career development. Feedback from your team leader, co-workers, clients/customers, and those who work with you on a regular basis who are usually in a good position to observe your performance can tell you what's working and what's not. You can compare their perspectives to how you see yourself.

> ## Feedback
>
> Response. Comments in the form of opinions about and reactions to something, intended to provide useful information for future decisions and development.
>
> Feedback is both a verbal and nonverbal process through which a person lets others know his or her perceptions and feelings about their behavior.
>
> Feedback is not about questioning another person's intentions. This will put the person on the defensive.

## What Feedback Can Do for You

Feedback will help you clarify. Feedback is useful in clarifying your skills, competencies, interests, and values. It will assist you in focusing on areas you need to develop. And as you invest your time and effort to improve yourself, feedback from others will help you measure your progress.

**Feedback from co-workers.** It is important to know how your co-workers see you. Co-workers are likely to be familiar with your job requirements, challenges, and stressors, and they know how you do your job. Moreover, they probably care that you perform well because you contribute to their success.

**Feedback from your team leader.** Team leaders view your effectiveness in the context of the team and the larger organizational goals. During feedback discussions, ask your team leader what he or she thinks are your strongest and weakest skills. A useful part of the feedback conversation could concern skills that your team leader views as most important to your position on the team.

**Feedback from internal and external clients/customers.** Knowing how well you are meeting the needs and expectations of your internal and external customers can alert you to problems so that you can address them before they become a crisis. In addition, by talking and listening to your customers, you can identify additional ways to support them.

As we have discussed, feedback is an integral part of interpersonal communication and building trust among team members. Within teams, members need to communicate to perform their tasks effectively so the team can accomplish its goals.

Team members need to know the proper use of feedback. There are ways to give it well and ways to receive it effectively. Giving and receiving constructive feedback is a learned skill that can be developed with planning, knowledge, and practice.

## Tips for Giving Feedback

Your team's ability to provide and receive feedback will often spell the difference between success and failure. Be clear about what you want. Do you want the other person to start doing something? Stop doing something? Do something differently? Or do more of something? Below are guidelines you can draw upon when planning your feedback to others.

- Recognize possible blind spots. Examine your own strengths and weaknesses to detect possible bias in the types of feedback you give to others. For example, are you so sensitive to criticism yourself that you are hesitant to point out ways your team needs to improve? Are you so task-focused that you provide little feedback about interpersonal relations?

- Be specific and separate the issue from the person. Instead of, "David, you are such a procrastinator and very inconsiderate." Try saying, "David, your monthly reports have been late for the last six months. What are you going to do to get future reports completed on time?" (Start doing.)

- Describe behaviors and support comments with evidence. People are most receptive to comments that are backed with rationale. For example, "Alice, I felt your behavior during my presentation was inappropriate. When I asked the group to pencil in the new figures in the budget, you slammed the report on the table, accusing me of not being prepared, saying you resented having to take meeting time to do my work. As I explained to the team, I was given the changes ten minutes before the meeting. Since you were late for the meeting, you missed my explanation." (Stop doing.)

- "Sandwich" negative messages between positive ones and avoid "but" and "however." Here is an example: "Sarah, I really appreciate the accuracy of your reports. *I do want less detail.* Instead of the three-page report you are currently providing me, please give me a one-page summary with pertinent facts. (Do differently.) I do like the format you are using and would like you to use the same format in all of your reports. (Do more of.) It is easy to follow and your grammar and editing are first-rate."

- Use "I" statements. With "I" statements you accept responsibility for your own perceptions and emotions as in "I see . . .""I think . . .,""My opinion is. . . ."

- Avoid "You" and absolute statements. "You" statements cause defensiveness, as in, "You should . . .""You ought . . .""You always. . . ."

- Describe the impact on you. "If you had called to let me know you wouldn't be attending the meeting, I would have asked John to take your place. (Do differently.) The client said he was very angry with me for not bringing an editor to the meeting to explain the copy changes. Because of this, I'm concerned that we may lose the account."

- Timing. Before the event, give feedback in the form of advice and support. Instead of saying, "Mary, given that your writing skills are elementary, hand me your report and I will edit it." Try, "Mary, I know how important the report is to you and how pressured you are for time. I can help you by editing it."

- Use the Planning Feedback Worksheet that follows to plan for a feedback session with another team member.

### Tips for Requesting Feedback

- Be specific in describing the behavior you want feedback on (for example, during meetings, communication style, follow through).

- Express appreciation.

- Tell the person how you plan to act on the feedback.

- Ask for any additional suggestions or input the person may have.

- Tell the person what specific actions or support you would find helpful.

- Use the Planning Feedback Worksheet to help you prepare a feedback session.

### Tips for Receiving Feedback

- Try to listen with an open mind. Pay close attention to what the person is saying. Don't try to justify or explain your behavior.

- Ask questions for clarification. Make sure you understand what is being said. If you are unsure that you understand, restate the message in your own words or ask questions about any aspect of the message that is not clear.

- Try not to be defensive. It is natural for people to experience some discomfort or defensiveness when hearing feedback, even when it is constructive. Some of what others say may be surprising to you. The hard part of learning how to grow professionally is getting people to tell you how you are perceived.

- Share your thoughts and feelings about the feedback you receive.

- Express appreciation for the information. Thank the person for being open and honest with you.

- Check the feedback with other people.

- Record the experience in your Career Development Journal (pages 86–87). Describe your thoughts and feelings and what you learned from the feedback. Note the development action steps you will be taking.

## Planning Feedback Worksheet

Plan a feedback session with one of your team members by answering the questions below.
Recipient's Name:

Describe the situation, issue, and behavior:

Describe what you want the recipient of your feedback to

Start doing                                                    Do more of

Stop doing                                                    Do less of

Do differently

Describe the positive outcomes the change of behavior could have on you, on the recipient, on the team, on others.

## Affirmations

Lack of recognition is demoralizing. Don't make the mistake of thinking that recognition is the sole responsibility of the leader. Being acknowledged by a peer with whom you work closely can be motivating. Often members are so focused on their next projects they neglect to express appreciation for a job well done. By acknowledging your colleagues' efforts, you affirm that their work is important and contributes to the team's success. Smart teams take time to celebrate both their efforts (the journey) and successes (the milestones and destination).

It's a fact that people like to be recognized and appreciated. Each person seeks appreciation in a different form. Some merely want a sincere acknowledgement. Others want a public announcement.

If you are unsure how your colleagues prefer to be recognized, ask them. Then you can show your appreciation in ways that are personally meaningful to them.

For ideas on how to express your appreciation for a team member see the Affirmation Feedback Worksheet on the following page.

## Affirmation Feedback Worksheet

Think about your team members and how their talents contribute to the team's success. Choose one or two teammates you think deserve special recognition and write one or more "praise paragraphs" below. Consider both task and relationship contributions.

Make your praise specific and relevant. Here are some "openers" that you can use to keep your praise specific.

- I'm impressed with . . .

- You're doing top quality work on . . .

- You really make a difference by . . .

- We couldn't have done it without your . . .

- I really appreciate your contribution to the . . .

# Exercise 6. Career Development Journal

Most people have plenty of experiences, but often they do not learn from them as fully as they could. Some people go from one activity to another without thinking about it or learning from it.

However, people can learn a great deal from what happens to them. A Career Development Journal provides a structural framework to help you identify useful learning experiences, develop an integrated learning plan, determine appropriate action steps, and measure your progress.

There are many different occasions on which journal entries should be made. Below are some examples:

- An experience, accomplishment, meeting, or discussion at work

- A major task force at work or any lengthy project

- Observations about self and others

- Immediately following a significant event

- At the end of each week or at the end of a program

- A new insight gained in a work assignment from feedback or an interpersonal relationship

Record any information about your developmental activities that is valuable to you.

The emphasis should be on reflection and insight, not on sentence structure or creative writing. Use the questions in the Career Development Journal Worksheet that follows to stimulate your thinking and guide you in your writing.

Some people find it difficult to take time for self-reflection. Initially, you too may find the discipline of keeping a journal restrictive and uncomfortable. If this is true, persevere. In the end you will find the process worthwhile and rewarding.

Keeping a journal can be a reinforcer. When you periodically review your journal, you will see how you have grown from your experiences and learning.

It will also be useful when reviewing your activities with the people you have designated for support and feedback.

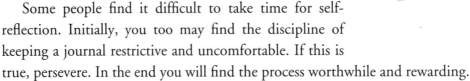

## Career Development Journal Worksheet

<u>Learning Activity</u>                                                                <u>Notes</u>

**What?**

What happened?

What was said?

Who did what?

What was the cause and effect?

What was the sequence of events?

**So What?**

What were the consequences?

What was the impact on people?

What were the outcomes, problems,
or benefits?

**Why?**

Why did it happen that way?

What were my motives?

What helped or hindered?

**What Did I Learn?**

What insights have I gained?

What will I do differently?

What are some possible options?

**What's New?**

What new thoughts, perceptions,
concepts, ideas, or values have surfaced?

What new awareness, feelings, attitudes,
motivations, skills, and behaviors have
I gained?

**What Progress Have I Made?**

My accomplishments

My projects

My learning and growth

My thoughts

# Exercise 7. Individual Success Versus Team Success

Members' motivations will influence the team's success. Team-oriented members who give precedence to the team's goals will adapt their behavior to accomplish the team's objectives. Conversely, members concerned predominantly with themselves will typically act in a manner that will build their personal power, advance their careers, or protect their knowledge and resources.

"Team and organization success demands individual sacrifice. It requires doing what is best for the team, as opposed to pursuing individual gain and credit. In baseball, a sacrifice fly or bunt may result in a player sacrificing his personal performance statistics to forward the team" (De Nijs, 2006, p. 49). This behavior characterizes a team orientation in which a person places greater importance on building the team than on receiving personal status and recognition.

The Team Player Assessment on the next page provides a way for you to evaluate your teaming skills. Scoring and Interpretation are on the following page.

## Team Player Assessment

How team-oriented are you? Do you know? Each of the following statements represents a quality of a valuable team member. Think about your team environment and the people with whom you interact. Read each statement below and indicate whether you already **Do** this **Well (DW)** or whether you **Need Practice (NP).** Scoring and interpretation are on the next page.

- [ ] 1. I participate fully in team discussions. I come prepared, ask questions for clarification, and contribute ideas.

- [ ] 2. I have been told that I am an active listener and maintain appropriate body language.

- [ ] 3. I understand my role and the roles of others on the team.

- [ ] 4. I know my company, its history, goals, core competencies, competitors, products, services, clients/customers, vendors, and market share.

- [ ] 5. I solicit and appreciate honest and direct feedback from others. I ask how they perceive my strengths, behaviors, and attitudes and how I can be a more effective team member.

- [ ] 6. I frequently go beyond what is required of me.

- [ ] 7. I take a personal interest in my teammates. I know their strengths, limitations, values, goals, and ambitions.

- [ ] 8. I am quick to recognize and praise others for their contributions and support.

- [ ] 9. I take personal responsibility for my career development. I identify challenging growth opportunities and develop personal goals that help the team achieve its goals.

- [ ] 10. I am willing to move out of my comfort zone and try new things.

- [ ] 11. I seek to manage conflict by focusing on information, issues, and facts, rather than on personalities.

- [ ] 12. I express my ideas and points of view, even when they differ from those of others.

- [ ] 13. I talk directly with a team member to resolve problems rather than complain to the team leader or other members.

- [ ] 14. I remain calm and rational, rather than angry and accusatory.

- [ ] 15. I am willing to subordinate my interests and tasks to the good of the team and its objectives.

- [ ] 16. I present the team's purpose and plans energetically to others outside the team.

- [ ] 17. I do not hoard. I share information and ideas.

- [ ] 18. Others describe my feedback style as thoughtful, supportive, and constructive.

- [ ] 19. I can clearly describe and define problems, analyze their cause(s) and significance, suggest new ideas, and propose and offer possible solutions.

- [ ] 20. My team trusts me. I walk my talk and follow through on my promises.

- [ ] 21. I am up-to-date on cutting-edge technology, processes, and industry trends.

- [ ] **TOTAL DWs**

## Team Player Assessment Scoring and Interpretation

Count the number of DW responses you selected and put that number in the total box.

| | |
|---|---|
| If the total is 17 or more | Congratulations. You are probably a team player who is willing to work hard at interaction and interdependence to assure your team achieves optimal performance. Keep up the good work. |
| If the total is 14 to 16 | You are doing a number of things right, but there are several areas you could work on to improve your teaming skills. |
| If the total is 13 or fewer | You are probably painfully honest with yourself and aware of your shortcomings in the area of teaming. You were more than likely picked to be a part of this team because you showed potential. Your contributions are important to the team's success. Discuss your score with your team leader, associates, coach, or mentor. Ask their advice and counsel on the areas you need to work on to change your behavior. |

## Your Critical Role

As a team member, you have a critical role in helping your team identify and address performance issues that hinder your team's growth and effectiveness, a role that those outside your team cannot fill. Why? Because . . .

- You have first-hand knowledge of what your team's problems are and what needs to be done about them.

- When you take an active part in the team's development, you feel responsible for setting goals, making the right decisions, generating creative solutions to problems, and supporting change initiatives.

- You have a stake in the outcome.

# Exercise 8. Stylemarks of High-Performing Teams

What does it take to go beyond performing to high performing? For teams to continuously add high value, there must be a drive for continuous improvement—a constant questioning of what they are doing and what they can do better in terms of service, quality, cost, products, volume, and profit. Members push themselves and other members to move forward and take action.

Although studies are ongoing, high-performing teams have five stylemarks (observable characteristics or attributes) in common.

**A High-Performing Team**

1. Drives innovation and thought

2. Is action-oriented

3. Influences change

4. Establishes collaborative relationships

5. Sustains interdependence and inclusion

The next worksheet takes you through the five stylemarks of a high-performing team. Questions are presented for your self-reflection and/or for discussion with your team members. Actions steps are suggested that you can take to strengthen your performance and benefit your team and organization.

# Stylemarks of High-Performing Teams Worksheet

## 1. A High-Performing Team Drives Innovation and Thought

A high-performing team looks beyond the present mental model and challenges the status quo. Its motto is to create the future, not react to it. Hermann Simon (1996), in describing high-performing companies' strategies and practices, said: "They are really good at tapping workers' creativity in many areas, large and small. . . . Most companies have huge repositories of undiscovered gold mines of creative ideas" (p. 211).

You may not think of yourself as innovative and creative, but you can be. With a little self-probing, you can activate your creative senses; you can learn to color outside the lines. The ability to promote innovation is very important. To stay ahead in today's marketplace, your organization, your team, YOU need to generate fresh ideas that will grow sales, raise standards, reduce costs, and/or improve services and operations.

Start with your current role. What two actions could you take that would make you more creative and innovative?

A.

B.

How would this benefit your organization?

## 2. A High-Performing Team Is Action-Oriented

High-performing teams and their members systematically try new approaches to find out how to move forward, and they take actions that produce results.

Think about your customers and your clients (internal and external) who use your services, products, and the ideas you deliver. What do they want or need that they are not receiving? If you are unsure, ask them. To give them what they need or want, what new approaches could you and your team take? Write your response below.

### 3. A High-Performing Team Influences Change

A high-performing team thinks ahead of the curve and is quick to seize new opportunities. Its creativity and confidence energize others to commit to the change and to help bring ideas to reality.

It is said that a leader is anyone who influences a person or team to help change something. Yes, you can affect change even if you don't hold an official leadership position or title. Think about your team and your organization. What situations need to be changed? Use your imagination and creativity and think "What if . . . ?" Describe a change that you think would benefit your team or organization and the strengths you bring (or could bring) to institute the change. Write your thoughts below.

### 4. A High-Performing Team Establishes Collaborative Relationships

A high-performing team actively cultivates a network of contacts at all levels in its organization, in customers' or clients' companies, as well as professional and industry organizations. Through networking, individuals and teams are able to establish and maintain relationships with others to exchange information and resources informally or formally in ways that are mutually beneficial.

How strong is your network? Give personal examples of times when networking has benefited (or could benefit) your team, your organization, and your personal and professional development.

## 5. A High-Performing Team Sustains Interdependence and Inclusion

A high-performing team sustains interdependence by removing the barriers that hold back less powerful participants from expressing their thoughts and feelings. It promotes inclusion by sharing roles and responsibilities with new and/or less experienced members.

### Beth's Story

Beth was selected among several high-potential candidates to join the team. She joined with high expectations of being a strong contributing team player, but within a short time began to question her fit. Beth describes the situation, as follows: "The team is effective in many ways. Goals are accomplished; projects are completed on time and within budget. What I am not comfortable with is that the older members are reluctant to share responsibilities with the newer members. Instead, they give the assignments to people who have already proven themselves. How can people grow if they are not given a chance to develop? When I suggest a new idea in a meeting, my input is not taken seriously."

To sustain interdependence and unity, you must persistently build bridges. Although you may be more comfortable working with team members with whom you have a history, it is important that you actively solicit and recognize ideas and encourage participation from all members.

A.  Brainstorm a list of actions the team could take that would support Beth's transition.

B. What do you personally do, or could you do, to promote interdependence and inclusion in your team?

## Exercise 9. Plan of Action and Milestones (POA&M)

There is an old proverb that says something like, "If you don't know which way you're going and which path you're taking, you'll end up going the same way you always have." The message is that real development doesn't happen until you recognize there is a reason to change, design and execute your plan, and determine how to measure your progress and make adjustments if you go off course.

Experience shows that it is better to focus on one development area at a time. Begin by reflecting on what you have learned about yourself. Next generate a list of potential development areas. When deciding what areas you want to develop, consider the following:

**The Present.** What do you need to begin doing right now to be a more effective team player? What specific behaviors do you want to change? What are you going to do differently?

Identify an area for action:

1. _____

**Your Strengths.** What do you do well that you could build on? Is there a strength that you are not fully utilizing that would further benefit the team and the organization?

Identify a strength that stands out that you could build on.

2. _____

**The Future.** What's on the company's and the team's horizon that will require new knowledge or a different skill set that you don't have and need to acquire? What do you need to know?

Identify a potential initiative that would require new knowledge or skills.

3. _____

# Plan of Action and Milestones (POA&M)

| Action Plan | Start Date | Milestone Dates | Completion Date |
|---|---|---|---|
| Action Area: | | | |

**Why did I choose this area?**

**What are my expectations for improvement?**

**What resources will I need?**

**How will I use it? To what extent will it make me a better employee? Benefit the team and the organization?**

**What potential roadblocks might get in the way? How will I overcome them?**

**How will I know I am successful? How will my team know? My organization?**

# V

# Suggested Development Activities, Exercises, and Resources for Each Stage

# Suggested Development Activities, Exercises, and Resources for Each Stage

## Initiating Stage

### Suggested Development Activities

- Get acquainted with each other and the task.
- Share information about interests, values, expectations, and capabilities.
- Develop team values.
- Determine purpose and mission.
- Identify stakeholders.
- Create structure, goals, and direction.
- Identify exercises and resources.
- Discuss recognition, motivation, and rewards.

### Exercises

- What's Important to Me, What's Important to You, PW, p. 56
- Team and Personal Values Worksheet, PW, p. 61

### Resources

- Get to the Point Books. Dallas, Texas. www.getothepointbooks.com
- *The Pfeiffer Library* (3rd ed.). (2003). San Francisco, CA: Pfeiffer.
- *Value*Base. (2001). Dallas, TX: The Ryan Group, Inc. (*Value*Base is an online assessment that will help you clarify and prioritize your values.)

## Conflicting Stage

### Suggested Development Activities

- Discuss what you can do to create and promote trust in your team.
- Define roles and responsibilities.

- Refocus on goals, breaking larger goals down into smaller, measurable action steps.

- Determine team members' personality types and develop a team profile to gain insight into your team's characteristics and members' similarities and differences. Your team's balance of similarities and differences will affect important key performance issues such as how your team will perform and how it will do what it sets out to do (results). This insight will help you and your team use and maximize the talents of all the team members.

- Develop effective communication and conflict resolution skills.

- Determine decision-making process.

- Celebrate accomplishments (even small ones).

### Exercises

- Talent Inventory Discussion Worksheet, PW, p. 62

- Trust Assessment Worksheet, PW, pp. 64–66

- Speak Up, Listen Up, Active Listening Assessment, PW, p. 74

- Think "We" Rather Than "I Versus You," Conflict Management Worksheet, PW, p. 79

### Resources

- Bower, S., & Blower, G. (1992). *Asserting yourself: A practical guide for positive change.* Reading, MA: Addison-Wesley.

- Burley-Allen, M. (1995). *Listening: The forgotten skill.* New York: John Wiley & Sons.

- Cartwright, T. (2003). *Managing conflict with peers.* Greensboro, NC: Center for Creative Leadership.

- CenterMark. (2001). Dallas, TX: The Ryan Group, Inc. (An online theory-based assessment.)

- Get to the Point Books. Dallas, Texas. wwwgetothepointbooks.com

- Kottler, J. (1994). *Beyond blame: A new way of resolving conflicts in relationships.* San Francisco, CA: Jossey-Bass.

- Mayer, B.S. (2000). *The dynamics of conflict resolution: A practitioner's guide.* San Francisco, CA: Jossey-Bass.

- Sharpe, D., & Johnson, E. (2003). *Managing conflict with your boss.* Greensboro, NC: Center for Creative Leadership.

- Stone, D., Patron, B., & Heen, S. (2000). *Difficult conversations: How to discuss what matters most.* New York: Viking.

- TeamMark. (2005). Dallas, TX: The Ryan Group, Inc. (TeamMark aggregates the CenterMark individual assessments results, along with the results of the team leader, and produces a report that provides insight into the team members' similarities and differences and how the team's balance of similarities and differences will affect important key performance issues.)

- *The Pfeiffer Library* (3rd ed.). (2003). San Francisco, CA: Pfeiffer.

# Stabilizing Stage

### Suggested Development Activities

- Develop and implement individual professional development plans.

- Develop constructive feedback skills.

- Use an assessment to determine the team's balance of task and relationship orientation, identify members' styles, and provide a profile of your team's unique style, its strengths, and growth opportunities. This insight will help you negotiate relationships and tasks so that your team and its members achieve mutually satisfactory goals.

### Exercises

- Giving and Receiving Feedback, Planning Feedback Worksheet, PW, p. 83

- Affirmation Feedback Worksheet, PW, p. 85

- Career Development Journal, Career Development Journal Worksheet, PW, p. 87

- Individual Success Versus Team Success, Team Player Assessment, PW, p. 89

- Plan of Action and Milestones (POA&M), PW, pp. 95–96

### Resources

- Get to the Point Books. Dallas, Texas. www.getothepointbooks.com

- Kirkland, D., & Manoogian, S. (1998). *Ongoing feedback: How to get it, how to use it.* Greensboro, NC: Center for Creative Leadership.

- *Team*Style. (2005). Dallas, TX: The Ryan Group, Inc. (*Team*Style expands on the model introduced in *Working* Styles. It presents a profile of your team's characteristics and helps you to determine your team's favored style, its strengths, and growth opportunities.)

- *The Pfeiffer Library* (3rd ed.). (2003). San Francisco, CA: Pfeiffer.

- *Working* Styles. (2001). Dallas, TX: The Ryan Group, Inc., 2001. (*Working* Styles is an online observable behaviors assessment that identifies a person's preferred style and his or her approach to task and interpersonal relationships.)

# Performing Stage

### Suggested Development Activities

- Take a progress check (for example, 360-degree feedback, client/customer surveys).

- Track and analyze emerging trends.
- Revisit both short- and long-term strategies and plans.
- Study and practice scenario (that is, what-if) planning.
- Review and update problem-solving processes.
- Create and implement service delivery agreements (SDAs).
- Encourage mentoring participation.
- Initiate cross-functional learning opportunities.
- Develop best practices.
- Instigate situational knowledge transfer.
- Conduct a relationship and task audit with another group in the organization.
- Develop inter-team skills by communicating with other teams; integrating work or tasks with other teams; developing joint decisions and solutions; and presenting shared outcomes.
- Consider change and its affects on individuals, teams, and organizations. Reflect and share your personal attitudes about change.
- Develop a change management strategy to help you and your team anticipate, plan, and implement successful change.

### Exercises

- Stylemarks of High-Performing Teams Worksheet, PW, pp. 92–94
- Plan of Action and Milestones (POA&M), PW, pp. 95–96

### Resources

- Davis, W. (2008). *Organizing change: A tabletop simulation.* San Francisco, CA: Pfeiffer.
- Davis, W. (2008). *The consultant's change toolkit.* San Francisco, CA: Pfeiffer.
- Get to the Point Books. Dallas, Texas. www.getothepointbooks.com
- Spencer, L.M., & Spencer, S.M. (1993). *Competence at work: Models for superior performance.* New York: John Wiley & Sons.
- *The Pfeiffer Library* (3rd ed.). (2003). San Francisco, CA: Pfeiffer.

# References

Chartier, M.R. (1976). Clarity of expression in interpersonal communication. In J.W. Pfeiffer & J.E. Jones (Eds.), The 1976 *annual handbook for group facilitators*. San Francisco, CA: Pfeiffer.

Cloke, K., & Goldsmith, J. (2000). *Resolving conflicts at work*. San Francisco, CA: Jossey-Bass.

De Nijs, E. (2006, March). Grace at work. *Training* and *Development, 60,* 49.

Hayward, K.J. (2003, March). The hierarchy of communications: A Wire One communication. www.wireone.com/html/learning/whitepapers/hireachy_of_communications.pdf.

Hirokawa, R.Y., De Gooyer, D., & Valde, K. (2003). Characteristics of effective health care teams. *Small group communication: Theory and practice*. Los Angeles, CA: Roxbury Publishing.

How employers view candidates. *The job outlook 2006*. Bethlehem, PA: NACE Publications.

Huszczo, G.E. (1996). *Tools for team excellence*. Palo Alto, CA: Davies-Black.

Kahn, M., Kroeber, T., & Kingsury, S. (1974). The I Ching as a model for a personal growth workshop. *The Journal of Humanistic Psychology, 14,* 39–51.

Katzenbach, J.R., & Smith, D.K. (1993). *The wisdom of teams*. Boston, MA: Harvard Business School Press.

Kormanski, C.L., & Mozenter, A. (1987). A new model of team building: A technology for today and tomorrow. In J.W. Pfeiffer (Ed.), *The 1987 annual handbook for group facilitators*. San Francisco, CA: Pfeiffer.

Luthi, J.R. (1978). Communicating communication. In J.W. Pfeiffer & J.E. Jones (Eds.), *The 1978 annual handbook for group facilitators*. San Francisco, CA: Pfeiffer.

Mehrabian, A. (1981). *Silent messages: Implicit communication of emotions and attitudes*. Belmont, CA: Wadsworth.

Pell, A.R. (1999). *The complete idiot's guide to team building*. Indianapolis, IN: Alpha Books.

Reilly, A.J., & Jones, J.E. (1974). Team building. In J.W. Pfeiffer & J.E. Jones (Eds.), *The 1974 annual handbook for group facilitators*. San Francisco, CA: Pfeiffer.

Rogers, C.R., & Farson, R.E. (1987). Active listening. In R.G. Newman, M.A. Danzinger, & M. Cohen (Eds.), *Communicating in business today*. Lexington, MA: D.C. Heath.

Scholtes, P.R. (1998). *The leader's handbook,* New York: McGraw-Hill.

Simon, H. (1996). *Hidden champions: Lessons from 500 of the world's best unknown companies*. Boston, MA: Harvard Business School Press.

Zajonc, R. (1963). Social facilitation. *Science, 149,* 269–274.

# About the Authors

**DARLENE DAVIS** specializes in the areas of organization effectiveness and human performance. She holds a master's of psychology from Antioch University and a bachelor's degree in social science from Marylhurst University in Portland, Oregon. Her areas of expertise encompass contemporary and classical theories of personality, personality development, and concepts used in understanding personality and behavior; the nature of attitudes and values; and social interaction, group dynamics, conformity, and leadership. Darlene is the creator of numerous assessments, developmental resources and tools, and leadership and coaching materials for individuals and teams.

**WAYNE DAVIS** is an author, strategist, and consultant in the areas of planning, change, and performance. His corporate experience and background include progressive roles as CFO and CEO. His client responsibilities cover domestic as well as international engagements in China, United Arab Emirates, Korea, Taipei, and others, serving a diverse client base in both the private and public sectors. Wayne works with senior leadership teams to improve their strategic performance and effectiveness. Wayne is currently authoring two works for Pfeiffer: a tabletop simulation for change and a program on executing change in the organization.

# Notes

# Notes

# Notes